M000092060

Let Go to Grow

Why Some Businesses Thrive and Others Fail to Reach Their Potential

Doug & Polly White

Palari Publishing
PO Box 9288
Richmond, VA 23227
www.PalariBooks.com
866-570-6724

First Edition

This book is a result of actual research, and as such, some of the people, companies, and circumstances have been altered for privacy. Any similarity to real persons, living or dead, is coincidental and not intended by the authors.

ISBN 978-1-928-66260-0

Library of Congress Cataloging-in-Publication Data

White, Doug, 1958-
  Let go to grow : why some businesses thrive and others fail to reach their potential / Doug and Polly White.
       p. cm.
  ISBN 978-1-928662-60-0 (hardcover)
  1. Business planning. 2. Decision making. 3. Entrepreneurship. 4. Success in business. I. White, Polly. II. Title.
  HD30.28.W445 2011
  658.4--dc22

                                        2011011721

Printed in the United States of America

Preface

Have you ever wondered why some businesses thrive and others plateau well short of their potential? The answer lies in how well each handles the inevitable challenges that every business faces as it transitions from micro to small and from small to midsize. The focus is on the role of the principal—the owner, the entrepreneur, the visionary who originally got the ball rolling. Specifically, we take a close-up look at how and why the skill set of the top person in the organization must change and grow as the business matures and reaches its potential.

Let Go to Grow is not about how to grow your sales or increase your market share. There are many other wonderful books on those topics. It's not about how to tap into the latest, greatest cutting-edge, buzz-word-of-the-month business trend. *Let Go to Grow* is about what makes the difference between strong, sustainable growth and blazing out like a shooting star or merely struggling along year after year, never quite making it to the next level. It's about how the journey of the leader's personal development determines whether the business will enjoy sustained success or suffer self-inflicted wounds that lead to a downward spiral of drama and chaos ultimately resulting in complete collapse.

Think that sounds a bit exaggerated? Think again. America is littered with entrepreneurs who had great ideas, great strategies, and great opportunities, but somehow, despite all of their blood sweat and tears, their enterprises never quite reached their full potential.

Let Go to Grow is about what happens to businesses and their owners as sales increase. It defines and examines the infrastructure that's necessary to sustain that growth. It's about how principals can avoid unwittingly suppressing the growth of their own businesses and how they can ensure that profits continue to flow as the business matures. Just as importantly, it's about how principals can maintain a personal life as their enterprise expands.

We're a bit different from the authors of many business books. We're not academics. Sure, we have academic credentials and we could choose to write many letters after our names; but we didn't learn the things about which we write in a management laboratory, a think tank, or a classroom. We're practitioners. We've lived them in the real world and we have the scars to show for it.

We've had the privilege of doing many different things over the past few decades. We've developed strategies for growth. We've seen those strategies succeed, and sometimes fail. We've made difficult tactical decisions—some good, some not so good. We've executed start-ups and bought businesses. We've fixed broken businesses and orchestrated turnarounds. We've grown businesses, improved their profitability and sold them. We've run companies, been responsible for the bottom line and managed employees—we've hired, fired, motivated, praised and disciplined them. In the course of our business careers, we've done many things right. We've done some things wrong. But most importantly, we've thought deeply about our experiences and we've learned from them. Now you too can benefit from our experiences.

We've worked in a very broad range of industries and with various types of companies as employees or consultants. These range from heavy-duty manufacturing companies to banks. We've guided Fortune 500 companies, helped privately-held start-up businesses, and advised government agencies.

Our expertise spans a very broad range of functional areas from finance to human resources, from operations to sales and marketing, and from customer service to IT. In short, we have had a very diverse set of experiences. Along the way, we've encountered some brilliant executives and some who were less so (to put it mildly), some outstanding managers and some who struggled mightily. Because of our broad experience, we've observed patterns of behavior—the similarities and differences—between those who succeed and those who do not. And what we've learned could put millions of dollars on your bottom line.

When we set out to write this book, we knew that we would build on our years of accumulated knowledge. We also believed in the old proverb—the truly wise man never stops learning. Therefore, we decided to broaden our perspective. We undertook the task of interviewing more than 100 key decision makers in a broad range of small and midsize businesses. We went to their offices, walked through their plants, and sat in their conference rooms. We asked questions, compared notes, and shared experiences. Most importantly, we listened and we learned. You and your business can benefit from the wisdom of the leaders with whom we spoke.

Much of what we heard resonated with our own experiences; but we also heard new thoughts and ideas that shaped our thinking. We debated what we heard with each other, spending countless hours arguing point and counterpoint. We honed our thinking.

As conclusions began to emerge, we didn't have an elite graduate school of business, a top-tier management-consulting firm, or a management laboratory with which to test and confirm our hypotheses. Accordingly, we took them back to the real world business leaders from which they had come to test validity. Again, our thinking was refined.

In the end, what we heard was great consistency. We learned that as businesses grow from micro to small and from small to midsize, principals face a consistent and predictable set of challenges. It's this insight that forms the basis of *Let Go to Grow* and that allows us to share with you, the passionate, motivated business owner or manager, how to navigate around the pitfalls that you will inevitably encounter as your business grows.

We are indebted to those who were generous enough to sit with us and share their experiences; those who allowed us to bounce our ideas off them and provided us with their thoughtful feedback.

We offer our sincere thanks to each one. Without their help, the insights of this book would not have been possible.

We guaranteed anonymity to those with whom we spoke in order to elicit complete candor. We agreed not to publish a list of the leaders with whom we spoke or the companies they run. Consequently, when we used an example that may reflect negatively on a company or an individual, we protected identities. All of our examples are real. A few are composites. We changed names and industries to conceal identities, but every example is either something that we experienced firsthand or something that was told to us by those who did. In cases where we did identify companies or individuals, we received their permission before doing so.

In most cases, the leaders we interviewed ran businesses that were very successful. With only a few exceptions, the owners of those businesses that weren't successful aren't around to interview. However, the principals of the successful businesses more often than not told us that they did struggle at some point with key transitions as they grew their companies. It was not unusual for successful midsize business owners to say, "You know, we almost lost the company."

Essentially every enterprise faces these challenges as they grow and transition. We don't think that it's possible to take the potholes and bumps out of the road. However, we can help principals and the companies they run to successfully navigate around them. We can help them learn to *Let Go To Grow*.

Table of Contents

Table of Contents

Part One:
Growth Requires Letting Go

Riverside Manufacturing began in the basement of George Carson's modest suburban home. George owned some woodworking equipment—table saws, joiners, planers, etc. He had made all of the cabinets and a lot of the furniture in his own home. He started taking in some project work on the side, building cabinets for some friends who were residential contractors. Initially he was just helping friends. George was a great woodworker with a passion for getting things right. Word began to spread. George was proud of the work he did. It was a labor of love. He kept his day job, but worked nights and weekends on his new business, a hobby really. Overhead was minimal, so his prices were very competitive. The requests for work from local homebuilders increased. Soon there was no time for the day job.

George hired a helper to handle the overflow. Soon the business outgrew the basement. George moved the business into rented space. A friend told George that he should incorporate the company, and so he did. Riverside Manufacturing was officially born. George beamed with pride, but he was also a little bit frightened. This was a big challenge. He purchased new equipment. Riverside's reputation grew, as did its revenue and its payroll. George hired more employees. The company was outgrowing its rented space. George needed to buy more equipment and he wanted to purchase a building.

There were some glitches, but eventually George secured a loan for the building and additional equipment. The business continued to thrive. Before long, the company built an addition on the building, hired more people, and bought more equipment. Riverside Manufacturing was flourishing.

George worked long hours. His days routinely started at 6 o'clock in the morning. Dinner was likely to be a sandwich or a pizza at his desk. He frequently burned the midnight oil. Weekends were often indistinguishable from weekdays. He missed some—really most—of his kids' games, but they understood. Dad needed to be at the office. George was working hard, but the work was fulfilling. He was succeeding. The fledgling enterprise was growing and it was profitable. George was able to take enough money out of the business to provide a nice lifestyle for his family. He just wished he could spend more time with them.

Riverside grew to a company with 40 employees. The employees operated the equipment. They built and installed the cabinets. They made sales calls and resolved customer service issues. They scheduled production, shipped product, sent invoices and paid bills. Overhead was still very low. There were no supervisors or managers. No one in the company really had that skill set. To the extent that there was any formal organizational structure, everyone reported to George.

Everyone knew his or her job. There was no process documentation. It wasn't considered essential and there was really no time for it. As George said, "We have good people, we just get it done." George was involved in every detail of the business. He made every important decision. He didn't need a lot of reports to know how things were going; the business was his life. Vacations were scarce. Time off was at a premium. Even when he was away, George was always reachable by cell phone. He was stretched thin to say the least.

Slowly, things began to change. The business began to stagnate. There were sales, but the profit seemed to have evaporated. The shop was a mess. Raw materials and work-in-process inventory were stacked up everywhere. To the untrained eye, it was hard to tell the difference between finished goods and scrap. Fire drills became the order of the day as workers scrambled to meet delivery schedules. Some of the contractors started to use other cabinet-makers who could deliver more reliably. Sales leveled off. Growth stopped. Riverside Manufacturing wasn't completely broken, but it wasn't running smoothly either. The company paid its bills, but too frequently, they were late. The company was struggling to make payroll. The business was in trouble.

George had been unwilling to let go of decision-making responsibility and he wouldn't delegate the hiring or management of any of the workers. To him, it didn't seem like a good idea. His employees were good at what they did, but he didn't have people that he trusted with that kind of responsibility. No one could make the important decisions as well as he did. No one cared about Riverside as much as he did. Could the company function if George weren't there to oversee every detail? How would he know what was happening in the bowels of the business if he couldn't touch the product and talk to every customer himself?

The workload had grown to massive proportions. George struggled under the burden—both physically and mentally. He knew that work was falling through the cracks and he anguished about it. Unfortunately, he was just simply out of capacity. He couldn't work more hours—they didn't exist. George's flourishing business was no longer growing. In fact, the business had begun to decline because George simply couldn't get to everything that was on his plate. Without knowing it, George had become the constraint to further growth. He was the bottleneck.

In our research for this book, we spoke with more than 100 small business owners and key decision makers. We heard stories of triumph and failure, excitement and frustration. We learned about the epic struggles associated with getting a business off the ground. We heard about the late nights and the weekend work that comes with starting a company. Sharon Dabney-Wooldridge exemplifies the challenges that these business owners overcame. She describes herself as a small woman, who started her cleaning business in 1986 with a vacuum cleaner, a sports car and a very big dream. More than two decades later, that dream is now a reality. Sharon forged her company, KleaneKare, from unimaginably hard work, tenacity and passion. For sure, founding a business is difficult. The statistics are stacked against a start-up. The fact is that most new businesses fail to survive for very long, let alone thrive.

Make no mistake; starting a new business is difficult at best. Still, as hard as starting a company is, it may be more challenging to grow a successful business. Through the morass of information we collected, one thing became clear. As businesses grow, there are many opportunities to get off track and many successful companies plateau well short of their potential.

As we started to examine the reasons for sales stagnation, some interesting observations began to emerge. We learned that the constraint to growth is generally not capital. It may not be easy, but with a good business plan and a lot of persistence, one can obtain financing. We found that the problem isn't usually a lack of good products or services. Most successful entrepreneurs have figured out how to deliver value to their customers. Market opportunity may limit global enterprises, but it doesn't derail the growth plans of small businesses. There are always new geographies, new market segments and new product categories to exploit.

No, we found that what most often limits the growth of small businesses is the inability or unwillingness of the principal to let go. To grow a business beyond the start-up phase, the principal must initially give up doing the primary work of the business. We spoke with entrepreneurs that just simply didn't want to do that. They loved what they did. They were passionate about their work. They did it very well and they didn't want to give it up.

For example, we met an outstanding interior house painter, an artist really. He loved to do complex faux finishes in higher-end homes. His work was magnificent. He had won awards for his creative finishes. He loved his work and he didn't want to give up painting. That's fine, but if the principal insists on spending most of his time with a paintbrush in his hand, doing the primary work of the business, growth will be limited. He's trying to do it all himself and he will soon run out of capacity.

If the principal can clear this first hurdle and delegate the primary work of the business to others, the business will continue to thrive. However, the time will come when sustaining further sales increases will be dependent on the principal's ability to relinquish day-to-day decision-making responsibility. In addition, the business owner will need to delegate the hiring and management of at least some of the employees to others.

ServPro is a franchise business that cleans up and restores buildings after fire and water damage. Andy Bahen, the owner of one of the ten largest ServPro franchises in the country, confessed that, "It took my wife seven years to get me off the truck and it was the hardest thing I ever did, not to personally oversee every job." If the owner insists on making every decision and managing the details of all of the work, the business will quickly plateau and further growth will not be possible. The principal has to delegate this work to others. While this step may seem to be a subtle difference, it is what we call the "Big Chasm." For many, it's more difficult than allowing others to do the primary work of the business. Riverside Manufacturing struggled because George couldn't navigate this transition.

Delegation is critical. However, worse than not delegating responsibility as the business grows, is doing so before establishing the proper groundwork. We heard numerous stories of companies that failed or almost failed because the owner trusted the wrong people and/or the proper systems were not in place to support delegation.

One company that has now become very successful almost had to file for bankruptcy protection as it was transitioning to a midsize structure. The owner delegated responsibility to an office manager who was not ready to accept it. Further, the owner didn't have documented processes in place to let the office manager know how she was supposed to perform her new duties. There were no appropriate metrics in place to let the owner know if things got off track. After making a number of mistakes, the office manager attempted to cover up the errors. By the time the owner discovered the cover-up, the business was perilously close to the brink.

Let Go to Grow chronicles the predictable challenges that all principals face as their businesses grow beyond the start-up phase. These are dangerous waters and few entrepreneurs have experience navigating them successfully. We've often heard parents say that children don't come with instruction manuals. Well, neither do most businesses. As anyone who has raised children knows, the skills needed to parent infants or toddlers are very different from those needed to guide a young person in their late teens or early twenties. In the same way, the skill set needed to operate a fledgling company where the principal does most of the primary work of the enterprise is very different from the skill set needed to be the CEO of a 250-person company with $125 million in revenue.

Growing a company requires a very diverse set of skills, and you will face many challenges as your business matures. As a result, many businesses fail or stagnate well short of their full potential. Bright and hardworking business owners can sometimes figure out how to make the necessary transitions through trial and error. But, the trials can be hard and the errors expensive. By using what we've learned over the years about growing businesses, you can avoid many common mistakes. We'll help you to navigate your business around the bumps in the road. We'll show you how to *Let Go to Grow*.

1: Why Grow?

Harvard Business School teaches that the primary objective of a business in our capitalist system is to create shareholder value. To oversimplify only a little, businesses increase shareholder value by growing the bottom line. To be sure, if a business has financial investors, there is a fiduciary obligation to grow the bottom line. You might think this is a no-brainer. Certainly all business owners would want to grow their enterprise. What we found might surprise you.

We know of a concrete contractor who has revenue of about $2 million per annum. The owner pulls enough cash out of the company each year to make a very nice life for himself and his family. He has time for a wonderful personal life and is able to pursue some hobbies that he loves. As a businessman, he is highly respected in his industry. Because he is honest, trustworthy, reliable, and good at what he does, there is usually more work than he can accept. Even when times are tough, he keeps his crews busy.

There is little doubt that he could grow the business significantly if he decided to do so. Growing the business would mean buying more equipment, hiring more people, probably working longer hours, and definitely delegating significant decision-making authority to new managers. The owner has decided not to take that path, at least not right now. All things considered, it's an incredibly reasonable decision. During the course of our research for this book, we interviewed many business owners who have made a similar conscious decision not to expand their companies any further. Growing their businesses is simply not something they wish to do.

However, as you might guess, most business owners do want to grow their companies. Some of the reasons include:

Increased Profits – The most obvious reason for growing a business is increased income and wealth creation for the owners. We all understand the calculation. If a business can deliver its products and/or services at a cost that is less than the price it charges, as sales grow, profits will follow. Isn't math wonderful!

We worked with a business that manufactured and sold electrical and electronic connectors. With sales of $30 million, the business had about 100 employees and was breaking even. Over the course of the next three years, sales increased by 50 percent while the fixed costs of the business were held constant. In this particular case, the number of employees increased by only about 20 percent. The increase was primarily in warehouse and assembly jobs. The result was unprecedented profits as much of the benefit from the sales increase fell straight to the bottom line.

As sales volumes increase, businesses can typically reduce other costs. For example, purchasing agents are often able to negotiate lower unit prices for raw materials when they buy in larger quantities. All else equal, when companies increase revenue, they make more money.

Resale Value – Many owners we interviewed expected to sell their company for a substantial profit. However, it's sometimes necessary to grow a business to be able to sell it at all. Many entrepreneurs plan to finance their retirement through the sale of their business. That's fine, but business brokers report that only about 25 percent of business owners who want to sell their companies are ever able to do so. One of the big reasons that businesses remain unsold is that they lack size and therefore profitability. Even if the

> **Business brokers report that only about 25 percent of business owners who want to sell their company are ever able to do so.**

business is large enough, the owner may not be able to realize a price high enough to finance the retirement he or she envisioned. In short, growing the business may be necessary to enable the owner's retirement plans.

Survival – There are times when a business needs to grow simply to survive. The old adage goes something like: You can only coast for an extended period if you are traveling downhill. Many have relied on this reasoning to argue that businesses have to grow or die. While this is not always true, there are certainly times when this is the case. Any business that has high fixed costs will have to grow to a certain size in order to have enough revenue to cover expenses. Failure to do so will result in bankruptcy.

For example, an entrepreneur started a corrugated box operation when he took out a loan to build a factory and purchase equipment. He hired several employees to operate the factory. In this case, the business had to generate revenue in order to pay employees and service the loan plus provide an income for the owner. Without growth, this business would not have been able to stay afloat for very long. Growing sales wasn't an option; it was a necessity.

Reduce Risk – Some businesses have only a few large customers. In such instances, owners often wish to grow their businesses to reduce risk. The goal is to spread the company's revenue over a larger customer base. This will reduce the risk associated with one large customer leaving. We worked with an organization that supplied temporary labor. The business enjoyed $4 million in revenue. Unfortunately, it went from very profitable to unprofitable when it lost one customer that represented more than $2 million of sales. There is wisdom to the old saying, "Don't put all of your eggs in one basket."

Giving Back – Still other business owners genuinely believe that the product or service they offer brings good into the world. It's not that they don't have capitalist motivations. They aren't driven by altruism alone. However, they do fundamentally believe that their business helps people and "doing more good" is a part of the motivation for expanding. Dawn Beninghove is the owner of

Companion Extraordinaire Nursing Network Inc., a company that provides home healthcare. The services that her company provides often allow people to stay in their own homes rather than having to relocate to an assisted living facility. She explained that her home healthcare company is, "A ministry, not a business." A large portion of her motivation for wanting to grow the enterprise is a sincere and heartfelt desire to help more people.

Upromise is another example of such a business. This company's mission is to help its members save money to pay for college. Members accumulate savings when they utilize selected financial services and purchase the products of partner organizations. When members buy products or services sold by partners, the partner agrees to rebate a portion of the purchase price into the member's Upromise account. As a privately held company, shareholders and employees alike saw this as important work that helped people make a better life for themselves and their families. They wanted to see the business expand, in part, because they wanted to help more people.

Leaving and/or Continuing a Legacy – Many business owners are motivated by wanting to leave a legacy. Marvin Bower was the patriarch of McKinsey & Company, which is now one of the preeminent management-consulting firms in the world. At one point in his career, Marvin gave up the opportunity to increase significantly his own personal wealth in order to put a management and ownership structure in place that would ensure the firm's growth for many years to come. Marvin's focus was not on creating addition personal wealth nor was it on building a monument to himself. His focus was on building a great firm.

When we walked into Darius Johnson's conference room at Consolidated Bank and Trust, one of the things that caught our eye was a picture of Maggie L. Walker. Maggie Walker was the black woman who founded the forerunner of this bank in Richmond, Virginia in 1903. Although there were exceptions, this was a time and a place where neither black people nor women were generally able to do such things. Her story is awe-inspiring to say the least. As we talked with Darius, one of the things that became obvious is that he felt almost a moral obligation to continue and build on the legacy handed down by Maggie Walker. It's easy to understand why.

Supporting the Next Generation – Often a business owner simply wants to build the company to a size that will support subsequent generations. A business that will support a family of four quite nicely may not be large enough to support the families of the second generation when they reach adulthood. Therefore, if all of the children are to derive their income from the business and maintain the lifestyle to which they have become accustomed, the business has to grow.

Ed Smith, a man with six children, faced this issue. Ed's grandmother founded Hello, Inc. in 1923. Bedridden, she was looking for something to do and decided that she could start an answering service. When his grandmother passed away, Ed's parents continued the business in their home. Ed took over the business shortly after his honorable discharge from the service in 1953. He grew it into a thriving company that provided a comfortable lifestyle for his family of eight. Out of necessity, Hello morphed into a number of corollary services over the years. As the years passed, the time came when five of Ed's six children wanted to work in the company. It was unclear whether the business would be large enough to support everyone. He described the problem of next generation overcrowding as having, "Too many snoots at the trough." When this happens, for everyone to be fed, you have to get a longer trough.

In the course of our research for this book, we learned that there are many reasons that business owners want to grow their enterprise. Whatever the motivation, as businesses grow, they will inevitably face challenges along the way. Fortunately, many of the challenges presented by growth are predictable and savvy entrepreneurs can take steps to mitigate their effects. We wrote this book to help the leaders of micro, small and midsize companies navigate the rough waters they will inevitably encounter as their businesses expand.

Lessons for Successful Growth

Do you want to grow your business? Are you happy with its current size, structure and profitability? You should make an explicit decision regarding whether or not you want to grow. It may be the right choice for you and your family to stop growing your business at its current size. But, make this a conscious choice! This should not be something that happens simply because you don't do the things necessary to allow your business to grow.

If you decide you want to expand your business, follow the advice laid out in the coming chapters. We can help you to *Let Go to Grow.*

2: A New Way to Classify Businesses

We set out to write a book to help owners and senior managers of micro, small and midsized businesses grow their enterprises profitably. However, to our surprise, the first thing we discovered in our research is that there is almost no agreement on the definition of a micro, small or midsized business.

You would think that the Small Business Administration would have a clear definition of small business. Well, they don't. Instead, they have, at last check, 44 pages of definitions. For example, if you are farming hogs and/or pigs, you are a small business until your annual revenue exceeds $0.75 million. However, if you are producing chicken eggs, the SBA labels your business "small" until your sales reach $12.5 million per year. Similarly, if your business is farming shellfish, it is "small" until yearly revenues eclipse $0.75 million. On the other hand, if you are catching shellfish in the wild, your business can grow to $4 million per annum before it will lose its small business moniker. As we said, these classifications go on for pages. While these definitions may be precise, they are of little value for our purpose.

After considerable discussion, argument, debate, and research, we concluded that classifying businesses by size (either revenue or number of employees) was both somewhat arbitrary and not particularly helpful. We were looking for breakpoints where the role of the principal had to change significantly. Depending on the type of business and industry, these breakpoints occurred at very different sales volumes or numbers of people. We needed a mechanism for classifying businesses that was not dependent on size. After all, it's a company's management structure, rather than its revenue or the number of people, that drives changes in the skill set needed by the senior manager.

To understand how two businesses of the same size can be fundamentally different, first, consider a well-known public figure who commands an average of $25,000 per speech. She is in such demand that she can easily book 200 appearances per year. The math isn't hard. Her $5 million-per-year business consists of herself and a personal assistant who handles all of the bookings and makes travel plans, etc.

Compare this to a $5 million-per-year distributor of electrical sensors and switches with whom we worked. This company had a President, a VP of Operations, a CFO, and a VP of Sales and Marketing. The two VP's and the CFO each had a small staff of people who actually executed the work of the business.

The public figure is the one who does the work of her business. She shows up for public appearances, delivers speeches, and autographs copies of her book. The personal assistant checks with her boss on any significant decision and simply executes the orders given. The public figure delegates no real decision-making authority. The most important factor in determining the long-term success of this enterprise is the principal's ability to maintain her celebrity status.

The president of the company that distributes sensors and switches, on the other hand, is actually managing people who manage the people who do the work of the business. Further, to be effective, the president must delegate large amounts of decision-making responsibility to the VP's and the CFO. For this business to be successful, the principal must demonstrate outstanding management skills and develop the appropriate business infrastructure.

The two businesses are the same size from a revenue perspective. However, from a management perspective they are clearly very different. The skills needed by the two principals are fundamentally divergent. Obviously, one would classify the two businesses differently in spite of the fact that they have equivalent revenue.

As a result, we have developed a classification system that looks at how a business is structured and managed rather than at its revenue or the number of employees in the business. At each classification level, the focus is on the job of the most senior person in the business—the principal. In privately-held companies, this will most often be the owner, although it needn't be. In publicly-held companies, the principal will be the most senior employee of the firm. We will focus on micro, small and midsize businesses in this book.

Micro Businesses – For our purposes, a micro business is one in which the principal does the primary work of the organization. Many law firms, consulting firms, and most start-ups fall into this category.

For example, we talked with the owner of a one-person company that sells baked products. The owner makes the sales calls, takes the orders, does the baking, delivers the product, and sends out the invoices. The success of this business is clearly a function of the owner's skills as a salesperson, baker, delivery person and administrator. This is a classic micro business. The wellbeing of the enterprise rests solely on the principal's ability to execute the work of the business. While a micro business may have some employees, the principal is still doing the primary work of the enterprise.

Obviously, in such a company the principal is involved in every aspect of the business. The business owner delegates nothing of significant importance. Even if the business has employees, they tend to be "helpers." The principal's efforts generate the preponderance of the revenue. The principal still makes every important decision. This structure has one key advantage. The principal completely controls the destiny of the firm. However, the downside is also clear. This model is unequivocally not scalable. The size of the business is inherently limited. Further, if the principal is not there, the work of the business stops.

Making the decision to remain a micro business is not necessarily a bad thing. Many people live happy, productive lives running such enterprises. But, if the principal wants to grow the business beyond a certain point, the management structure must change.

Micro Business: The principal does the primary work of the business.

Small Businesses – Small businesses are next in the progression. The defining characteristic at this level is that the principal is managing people who do the work of the business. As an example, we interviewed the owner of a company that provides security services to businesses (burglar alarms, smoke detectors, etc.). The business employs several installers, two salespeople, office workers that handle billing and other administrative tasks, as well as a small group of employees that monitor the systems. Each of the employees reports directly to the principal. He is managing people who do the work of the business.

In a small business, the principal may still engage in the primary work of the enterprise, but those whom the principal manages generate the preponderance of the revenue. The key success factor for small businesses is the management skills of the principal. This is a fundamentally different skill set than the one required to succeed at the micro-business level. One of the huge issues faced by businesses making the transition from micro to small is how well the principal can transition from "Doer" to "Manager." It's not always easy and many businesses have failed in this transition.

Once a company is a small business, the principal will have delegated responsibility for doing the primary work of the business to multiple employees. Because there are more people doing the work, the business can deliver larger volumes. This will enable the organization to grow well beyond the size it could sustain as a micro business. However, the number of people that the principal can effectively manage still inherently limits its size. While the principal will no longer be doing the primary work of the business, he or she will have retained responsibility for all of the important decisions. The employees are essentially following the orders of the principal. This means that if the principal is absent, the business will grind to a halt in relatively short order.

We worked with a construction firm that had 10 employees and a small business structure. Everyone reported to the principal and he made every significant decision. When the owner took his annual week of vacation, the company simply shut down. No one worked.

Many business owners will make a conscious decision not to grow. They choose to remain in a small business structure. One of the primary reasons for their reticence to grow further is that doing so would require delegating decision-making responsibility, which means giving up control. This is a very scary step for many small business owners.

Another limitation of owning either a micro business or a small business is that it is often difficult to sell. At both levels, the business owner continues to make every important decision. Often the principal has every major relationship with customers and suppliers alike. Therefore, the business is, in effect, the owner. He or she drives all of the revenue. Without the owner, there isn't much of value to sell. Under certain circumstances, the business may be salable. Still, the owner will most likely need to sell the business to someone with significant experience in the industry, someone who can immediately make all of the important decisions.

> **Small Business:
> The principal manages employees who do the primary work of the business.**

Midsize Businesses – When a business transitions to midsize, the principal is managing managers. It is those managers who manage the people who do the work of the business. The principal must now manage the enterprise. This requires a fundamentally different skill set than the one required to perform the primary work of the company (as in a micro business) or the skill set required to manage people who do the work of the organization (as in a small business).

For example, we worked with a manufacturer and distributor of computer equipment. The CEO's direct reports were a VP Finance, VP Sales, VP Marketing, VP Human Resources, and VP Operations. Each VP had a staff. It was these staff members (or in some cases their direct reports) who actually did the primary work of the business.

Several fundamental changes occur when a business transitions from small to midsize. First, the company is now dependent not only on the management skills of the principal, but also the management skills of the principal's direct reports (in this case the VPs). This means that it is critical for the company to have good managers in place.

Second, to be effective at this level, the principal must delegate day-to-day decision-making and people management responsibility to the new layer of management. To be sure, the principal will still be involved in setting the strategic direction of the enterprise and in the larger decisions that will have a major impact on the company's performance. However, for the company to flourish at this level, he or she must empower his or her direct reports, which means relinquishing authority.

The principal's primary job becomes working *on* the business rather than working *in* the business. Letting go of decision-making authority can be difficult. Our research led us to the conclusion that for many principals the transition to being a successful midsize company is more difficult than transitioning from a micro to a small company management structure.

Letting go is critical. In fact, the acid test for a successfully run midsize company is whether the business would continue to function normally if the principal were to leave for two or three months? A company is operating as a midsize business only when the answer to this question is an unqualified "Yes." Admittedly, during the principal's absence, employees won't make strategic decisions, but the day-to-day operation of the business will go on.

Third, while the principal must remove him or herself from the day-to-day operation of the business, he or she can't lose touch with what is going on in the enterprise. Therefore, the principal will need to put process in place to ensure that work continues consistently across the organization. Developing documented processes isn't very sexy, but it is the only way to ensure consistent execution across a sprawling enterprise over time.

Finally, the owner will need to develop a comprehensive set of metrics. These will allow the principal to monitor the health of the company without personally being involved in every decision. In this way, if an issue arises, the principal will be aware of it quickly and can act accordingly before the problem becomes worse. If a principal only finds out about a problem when it shows up in the Profit & Loss statement (P&L), it's too late. The damage has already been done.

Midsize Business: The principal manages an enterprise.

Large Businesses and Conglomerates – The focus of this book is on micro, small, and midsize businesses. However, for completeness, we will extend our thinking to large businesses and conglomerates as well. In a midsize business, the principal will have delegated much of the day-to-day operation of the business to the functional managers who report to him or her. However, real P&L responsibility still rests with the principal and the principal remains the only General Manager.

A business has moved from midsize to large when the principal has delegated P&L responsibility to a series of General Managers. However, at this level the company will still essentially be in only one business. We worked with a manufacturer of industrial sewing machines that exemplifies the definition of a large business. The president had the following direct reports:

o General Manager of Operations — This person was responsible for three factories each of which produced sewing machines and spare parts (in the US, the UK and the Netherlands). The company sold the machines and parts to the sales offices at predetermined transfer prices. The GM of Operations was responsible for managing the P&L's of each of the three factories, which also included R&D functions for the machines they produced.

o General Manager of Sales and Service — This person was responsible for the company's five sales and servicing offices in the US, the UK, France, Germany, and Hong Kong. Each of these sales offices was set up with a separate P&L and purchased the machines and spare parts they sold from the respective factories at the predetermined transfer price.

o General Manger of the Independent Channel — The independent sales and service channel was a separate P&L. It consisted of a series of manufacturer's representatives that covered countries where the company did not have direct representation. The Manufacturer's Reps purchased machines and parts directly from the various factories.

o Chief Financial Officer — The CFO was responsible for a cost center that provided administrative support for the balance of the business.

To be sure, the president was still responsible for the overall profitability of the company. However, he delegated P&L

responsibility to three of his direct reports. Furthermore, the company remained in only one business: the manufacturing, sales, and servicing of industrial sewing machines.

When the P&L managers reporting to the principal are in fundamentally different businesses, the company has moved into the conglomerate classification. For example, the president of the industrial sewing machine company described above had four peers, each of whom reported to the Chief Executive Officer. The other four businesses were a manufacturer of bowling equipment, a series of bowling centers, a manufacturer of equipment for the bakery industry, and a manufacturer of golf products. Taken together, the CEO was managing a conglomerate because reporting to him were a group of General Managers each with P&L responsibility, managing companies in fundamentally different businesses.

It is worth noting that within a large business or a conglomerate, there may be a number of midsize, small or even micro businesses embedded in the corporate structure. As these embedded businesses grow, their principals will face the same challenges as their independently owned counterparts. Even if a larger parent owns and runs the entities, these principals will have to let go if their businesses are to grow successfully.

We defined three very specific types of businesses in this book: micro, small, and midsize. These definitions draw clear lines of distinction between each. As you would expect, in the real world, things aren't quite so clean. There are hybrids. For example, we spoke with a company in the construction industry that has two crews, each managed by a supervisor. The supervisors report to the owner. The principal rarely does the physical labor associated with the construction work. The crews do that. The supervisors are managing the workers, but they are working supervisors who physically do the work themselves. From this prospective, the contractor would appear to be a small business or perhaps an emerging midsize business, because the supervisors both manage workers and do the primary work of the business. On the other hand, estimating (assessing how much it will cost to deliver each job and deciding what price to quote) is clearly part of the primary work of the business as well. However, the owner reserves this job exclusively for himself. Therefore, from this perspective the business would seem to be a micro business.

In fact, the business is a hybrid. That's because the owner must exhibit a combination of those skills required of the principal of micro, small and midsized businesses. It is the owner's skills as an estimator that will, in large part, determine how much work the company has and whether it will make money doing the work. This is clearly a skill associated with the principal of a micro business. However, the success of the business will also depend on the owner's skill as a manager since he is managing the supervisors who do part of the primary work of the business. This is clearly a small business skill. The owner has also delegated some significant decision making authority to his supervisors. For example, the supervisors have hiring and firing authority. So, from this perspective, the owner is exhibiting a skill associated with being the principal of a midsize business.

The fact that some businesses don't fit cleanly into one category is not a significant concern. The important question is what skill set does the principal need to master for the business to succeed? Particularly as businesses are transitioning their management structures from micro to small or from small to midsize, the principal may need to demonstrate skills normally associated with more than one of the business types. We refer to businesses that are in the process of transitioning from a micro to a small business structure as emerging small businesses. Similarly, we describe businesses that are in the process of transitioning from a small to a midsize business structure as emerging midsize businesses.

Lessons for Successful Growth

What type of business do you have? Identify your place in the business hierarchy so that you can prepare for the challenges that lie ahead.

- **Micro** – The principal does the primary work of the business

- **Small** – The principal manages employees who do the primary work of the business

- **Midsize** – The principal manages an enterprise

For a business to grow successfully, the principal must develop a new and very different set of skills at each transition (from micro to small, and from small to midsize). This book examines the skills needed at each of the two critical transitions. We will describe what happens if the principal doesn't master the new skills, and what he or she can do to ensure that the skills are successfully developed.

Part Two:
Running a Micro Business

A micro business represents the simplest of all structures. Therefore, it makes sense to begin our consideration of how to run a micro business by starting with the very core of the enterprise. Broken down to the least common denominator, successfully running a business, micro or otherwise, is about figuring out what to do and then getting it done. It's just that simple...and that complex. Both figuring out what to do and getting it done, admittedly, can be fraught with challenge. But, at its core, this is what you need to do to operate a successful business.

As you will remember from the last chapter, in a micro business the principal is personally engaged in doing the primary work of the business. "Getting it done" is a critical part of the principal's job description. Often there just isn't anyone else. Delegation isn't an option. It's important to remember that the primary work of the business will expand to include all activities that are necessary to run the company. In fact, we advise would-be entrepreneurs not to start a new venture simply because they want to do the primary work of the business. There is a lot more to running a widget business than just making the widgets.

Consider our friend, Stuart Chalifoux. Stu owns and operates a very successful tax accounting service. Preparing his client's tax returns and representing them before the IRS, when necessary, are a part of the primary work of Stu's business. However, he also keeps his own books, attends networking meetings, follows up on referrals, and cultivates relationships that he hopes will result in new clients. To be blunt, in order to maintain a successful business that can pay his salary, Stu has to sell. Without this effort, revenue would shrink to an unacceptably low level. The tax work is critical, but it isn't the only required activity.

In a micro business, the principal's skill set and his or her motivation make the difference between success and failure. Does the principal have the ability to do the work and the will to do it? If the principal has a weakness in either area, is there a workaround?

There are many seminars offered with the primary purpose of improving or developing specific abilities of the attendees. For example, classes are readily available to help people improve their skills in areas such as selling, communication, and the use of various software packages such as QuickBooks, PowerPoint, Word or Excel. In fact, many professions require continuing education to ensure that practitioners keep their knowledge and skills up to date.

If motivation is the issue, a good business coach can help an entrepreneur develop daily action steps. Many business professionals find reporting their progress to a coach creates accountability that can be an excellent motivator. However, if an entrepreneur is significantly lacking in either the skill set needed to succeed in a particular endeavor or the motivation to get the work done, it is probably best to consider alternative employment. There is wisdom to the old adage that you can't make a silk purse out of a sow's ear. You shouldn't try.

Beyond executing the primary work of the enterprise, the principal of a micro business has the responsibility to figure out what to do. This can be broken down into two additional responsibilities: making tactical decisions and developing strategy. For our purposes, strategy involves those decisions that set the long-term direction of the enterprise. Tactical decisions, on the other hand, are those day-to-day choices. They may not require massive amounts of prior planning, but the principal must make them in the course of executing the strategy.

Let's use taking a vacation as an example. Decisions that require prior planning would represent strategy. They would include things such as deciding when to take the vacation, where to go, who to invite on the trip, where to stay while visiting, and whether to get there by taking a plane, train or automobile. Having decided to drive, tactical decisions would include things such as deciding where to stop for gas and lunch along the way. To some, these are, perhaps, important decisions, but generally don't require a lot of planning prior to the trip.

So far, we've identified three primary activities that the principal needs to execute to run a successful micro business: (1) doing the primary work of the business, (2) making tactical decisions, and (3) developing a strategy. As the chart below indicates, the principal should only be engaged in doing the primary work of the company while it is a micro business. Once the business transitions to a small structure, the owner will delegate much of the work to others. The principal will continue to make tactical decisions of importance through the small stage, but will need to delegate those decisions to others when the enterprise becomes midsize. Conversely, the principal will maintain primary responsibility for setting the strategy through the business achieving midsize status.

Principal's Responsibilities

	Micro	Small	Midsize
Doing the work of the business	✓		
Make tactical decisions	✓	✓	
Develop strategy	✓	✓	✓

In the balance of this section, we will cover:

- Doing the primary work of the business

- How to make tactical decisions effectively

- What it takes to develop strategies that work

3: Doing the Primary Work of the Business

Many entrepreneurs started their companies because they have a passion for the primary work of the business. For example, a nurse started a home healthcare business after she couldn't hire appropriate care for her dying father. She knew that she could do an outstanding job of providing a much-needed service. The owner of a successful wine shop opened the doors because he loved wine and discovered that he had a gift for helping his customers find a bottle they would enjoy at the right price point.

Some business owners start their enterprises because they become frustrated with their employers. They want to be their own bosses and believe that they can do a better job than that "idiot" they currently work for. Others choose to work for themselves when they are laid off or fired. Finding themselves unemployed, they decide to "buy themselves a job." This carries with it the attendant benefit of not having to worry about being laid off or fired ever again. Many hope for economic gain. They expect that they can make more money working for themselves than they could working for someone else. Owning your business means you determine your own destiny and compensation. There is at the least the opportunity to create your own income, without predefined limits.

Whatever the motivation, hundreds of thousands of people decide to start a new business each year. Typically, the new enterprise will be a micro business. This means that the owner will be doing the primary work of the business. In many cases, the owner will be the only employee of the company at inception.

Starting a new business will take a lot of homework and preparation, but here are a few key points to remember.

- Possess the requisite skills to do the primary work of the business (or if you possess only some of the required skills, you can partner with someone who has a complementary skill set)

- Recognize the need to perform ancillary functions

- Realize that growth means you will have to let go of doing the primary work of the business at some point

Possess the Requisite Skills

Nancy got the bad news on a Friday afternoon. She felt like she couldn't breathe. She'd been laid off. After twelve years of service as an accounts payable specialist with a well-known manufacturing company, Nancy's boss told her that her services were no longer required. She had become another victim of the recession. She couldn't think. At first, she felt nothing, a sort of numbness and disbelief. Then the emotions started to roll in.

Her first emotion was anger. How could they do this to her? She'd been a model employee, a team player, and a good accounts payable specialist. She knew that with the recession the company had to reduce costs. Even so, was this the thanks she got for her loyalty?

The next wave brought fear. She had obligations—bills to pay—she was a single mom. Her children depended on her. The two months of severance she received was better than nothing, but she knew she'd run through that in short order. She needed to find a job, and quick. Unfortunately, the economy was the worst she'd ever experienced.

The next emotions to take hold were hopelessness and desperation. Nancy knew it would be difficult for a woman of her age to find work in the best of times. It was likely a near impossibility under the current economic conditions. She wondered what would become of herself and her family. She sank into a dark depression. Sleepless nights were followed by days where she felt almost paralyzed. Nancy just didn't know what to do.

Then in her darkest moment, she saw a glimmer of hope. There was a business for sale. It was a franchise business that made signs. It produced everything from plastic banners to tradeshow displays. She'd need two employees, one person to sell the signs and one to make them. She would manage the business and best of all, as the owner, no one could fire her.

Challenges remained. For example, where would she get the capital to finance the business? She was good with numbers. She could figure this out. Her research brought her to the Small Business Administration (SBA). Much negotiation led to a $150,000 SBA loan. The bank required Nancy to pledge her house as collateral, but for the moment, that seemed a small price to pay for independence.

Nancy found some space to rent. She paid the hefty franchise fee, took delivery of the equipment and went to the training session that came with the agreement. She hired two employees. One was an experienced sign maker who knew how to run the equipment. The other was a salesperson. She negotiated a fair salary with each and launched her new business, Signs R Us.

Things moved a bit slowly at first. Nancy was paying herself and her two employees from the cash reserve generated by the SBA loan. As the president, Nancy held company meetings each morning at 9:00 a.m. to discuss every detail of the business with her staff. Sometimes the meetings went for two hours or more. There were some opportunities, but sales weren't coming in quickly enough.

Nancy started attending networking events to drum up business. This generated a large number of meetings for coffee. Nancy became a regular at every coffee shop in town. The people she met were good folks, but most of them didn't need any signs. Sales continued to lag. She had to do something.

Nancy turned her mind to happier tasks. She hired a new sales-person. Again, she negotiated a fair salary. Perhaps this would lead to the ramp in business that she so desperately needed.

Nancy discovered more problems with her business plan. The market was saturated. There were many people in the area who owned sign-making businesses. They produced a product identical to Signs R Us. Nancy learned that the space, on which she had signed a long-term lease, wasn't ideal. Given its location, there was little walk-in business. The building had another problem. Car wraps were among the most profitable parts of the business. Unfortunately, you had to bring the car or truck inside a garage to do this work properly. Signs R Us had a long-term lease on a building with no such space.

Finally, the equipment began to malfunction. There was no way to fulfill the few orders that the business had. No completed orders meant no revenue. The franchise agreement provided for service, but that was expensive and the nearest technician was a couple of hours away. Several weeks and a few thousand dollars later, the machine was fixed. The company couldn't afford this expense, but there was no alternative.

The new salesperson's climb up the learning curve was a slow one. Sales weren't coming quickly enough. Cash began to get tight. The company had burned through the small cash reserve and now had to survive on what it earned. Nancy began to give her employees smaller checks than had been agreed. She paid herself very little. Then she missed a loan payment. At home, Nancy's bills were mounting. She was falling behind. She maxed out her credit cards. Ultimately, her access to credit was turned off and so was her cable TV and home phone.

The bank that made the SBA loan began to ask for meetings. Nancy owed them money and they wanted it. Nancy developed plans to show the bank that her business was viable. But, the sales didn't materialize. Desperate, Nancy began to sell her receivables to generate cash. Unfortunately, she received only a fraction of their value. It wasn't enough to get her current, but she did manage to get her phone turned back on at home. The money wasn't enough. She still wasn't making her loan payments on time. Then Nancy got the news. At the end of one of their frequent meetings, the bank informed her that it was going to have her home appraised.

The process took longer than might have been expected. Sadly, extra time is not necessarily a kind thing. It prolonged the struggling, but had no impact on the outcome. The bank called the loan. Nancy declared personal bankruptcy. Signs R Us was no more.

This is a tragic story. Unfortunately, we see this all too frequently. In retrospect, the outcome might have been predictable from the start. Prior to starting Signs R Us, Nancy had never worked in the industry and had, at best, a cursory knowledge of how it worked.

The principal of a micro business needs to be very qualified to perform the primary work of the business.

She never really learned to operate the sign-making equipment. Although she tried, Nancy lacked the skill set to sell the product effectively. The primary work of the business was selling and making signs. Nancy could do neither.

It may sound like remedial counsel to say that before starting a micro business, the owner should ensure that he or she can do the primary work of the business. Yet, we ran into many people, who like Nancy, charged headlong into an entrepreneurial venture without thinking this issue through clearly. It is unusual for a startup business to succeed if the owner(s) lacks the ability to do the primary work of the business. There are several reasons for this.

First, an owner who does not do the primary work of the business is overhead. That means you are not necessarily critical to your own business! The business would need to generate significant cash flow to carry this kind of overhead. In Nancy's case, it was unlikely that one salesperson could have generated enough income to support this cost.

Second, as a manager, Nancy was responsible for those who were doing the primary work of the business. That's a tall order when you don't know how to do what they are doing and have little to no experience managing the function. For example, never having sold or managed a sales function, Nancy had no idea how to construct a compensation system. Paying her sales people a straight salary, rather than commission, was probably not the best idea. Salespeople most often receive commission rather than a salary. This provides incentive for them to produce and reduces the company's costs in the event they don't.

Further, she should have been more involved in supervising sales calls. Nancy should have held her salesperson accountable for making a certain number of cold calls per week. This should have resulted in a specific number of sales calls. Some percentage of the sales calls must result in closed business. By tracking the progress of prospective customers through the sales process, Nancy could have focused attention on areas that needed improvement.

Finally, Nancy's lack of knowledge about the industry caused her to make several critical mistakes. For example, she didn't realize that the sign-making capacity in the area greatly exceeded the demand. She didn't know that she should have rented a space that would generate walk-in business. Nor was she aware that the rented space should have provided her access to a garage where she could have installed car wraps.

It may sound remedial, but if you are going to open a micro business, you had better have the skill set and the experience to do the primary work of the business. In recent years, it's become popular to say that business people need to "confront the brutal facts." That's good advice. Imagining that things will work out while ignoring major issues is a recipe for disaster. The right time to confront the brutal facts is before committing your life savings to a business about which you know little or nothing.

Recognize the Need to
Perform Ancillary Functions

Theresa loved to cook and she was good at it. Her specialty was salsa. It was fantastic. She won awards for it. Theresa's salsa was the hit of every church potluck dinner. She bottled her salsa and gave it to friends and family during the holidays and at birthday celebrations. These gifts always received rave reviews.

Theresa was passionate about making salsa. It filled her with joy. For years, people had told her that she should go into business making salsa. So, finally, she did. She set up production in her kitchen, had a jar professionally designed and bottled the first few batches of "Theresa's Extra Special Salsa." She called on specialty food shops in the area and after tasting the product, they agreed to carry it. A couple of Mexican restaurants agreed to serve her salsa if she would put it in five-quart jars, which of course she did. One even put a sign in the window that proclaimed, "Theresa's Extra Special Salsa served here!" The first time Theresa saw it, tears of pride welled up in her eyes.

Six months into the venture, the business was growing rapidly. Theresa was working 14-hour days, six days a week. She tried to take Sundays off, but she rarely succeeded. She still made every ounce of her beloved salsa. She didn't mind this. What she minded was all the other stuff. She had discovered that there was a lot more to running the business than making salsa. On Monday, Wednesday and Friday she closed the kitchen at 2:00 so that she could hit the streets with her product. She was the salesperson and the delivery driver.

She handled accounts payable and entered information into QuickBooks. She squeezed in writing checks and doing the book-keeping whenever she could find the time. Theresa produced invoices in the evening and mailed them on her way to make deliveries. When the checks were late, she became the collections department. She made those calls in the morning. She hoped to catch people before they had time to get in a bad mood.

Theresa went to bed late and got up early. Most often, she started the next day the way she had ended the last one—exhausted. She still loved making the salsa; but the rest of the work, not so much. Theresa had gotten more than she'd bargained for.

If you are going to start a company, you had better want to run a business. As a micro business, you will have more to do than just the primary work of the enterprise. For example, you will need to set up a bookkeeping system and administer it. You'll likely need to advertise and market your business. You will perform administrative functions such as accounts receivable, accounts payable, and payroll. You'll probably need some sort of IT infrastructure and the list goes on.

These functions are ancillary to the core business. However, they are not unimportant— quite the opposite. One of the most frequent needs we find in small businesses concerns their financial statements. In order to provide the type of information needed to make

If you are going to start a new company, you had better be prepared to run a business—not just focus on the work you enjoy.

good business decisions, the financials need to be recast. More than one small business has gone bankrupt because the owner didn't have a clear picture of the company's financial situation and lost sight of cash flow. Getting these ancillary functions right is critical to the survival of any business.

Further, to be truly successful you'll have to focus on building a system that others can repeat. If you are successful and the enterprise grows, the principal will have to let go of doing the primary work of the business. If what you really love is making salsa, our advice is, "Do not start a business." If you believe you will spend your days chopping tomatoes and jalapeños, you will be disappointed. Instead, seek a position in a restaurant where they appreciate good salsa. Alternatively, if the business can afford it, find a partner or an outside company to do the work that you don't enjoy.

However, there are several ancillary functions that you probably should outsource. In fact, it is likely that the first help a new firm hires will come from people who aren't employees at all. For example, many small businesses will hire an attorney to help establish a legal entity, and a CPA to set up the books and check them periodically. They might hire a Web design firm to set up their fledgling company's Web site and engage an IT company to establish a computer network. Without exception, the hourly rates charged by the external companies aren't cheap. Employees doing the same tasks would cost less per hour. So, when is a company better off to perform a function internally and when should it employ the services of outside firms? In other words, when should you rent rather than buy the service?

Key business functions should be outsourced when:

- A specialized skill is required and that expertise doesn't exist within the company

- There is not enough of this kind of work on an ongoing basis to justify hiring an employee to do it (full-time or part-time)

- The time and cost associated with training someone to do the work internally is not justified

- The task is not core to the success of the business and doing it distracts from higher value tasks

The rent-versus-buy decision generally boils down to cost. In the long run, the real question is whether it is less expensive to outsource the service or to hire someone to perform it in-house? There is an exception to this rule. Sometimes there is a benefit to having an objective third party perform a service. For example, there may be someone in the company capable of moderating a brainstorming and problem-solving meeting. Even so, at times an outside moderator might be more effective. As we say in the South, "They don't have a dog in the hunt." In other words, they don't bring baggage into the meeting.

Success Means Letting Go

Now two-years old, Theresa's Extra Special Salsa was doing fairly well. It had grown. The revenue that it was generating paid the bills—well almost. Theresa had to dip into her personal savings to cover the household bills only once in the past six months—a big improvement from the early days.

Then it happened. Theresa was dicing tomatoes when the phone rang. The caller identified himself as a buyer from a regional grocery chain. Would she be interested in having his store carry Theresa's Extra Special Salsa? This was her big break! Of course, she was interested!

A meeting was set up. Talks continued over the next few weeks. Theresa sent samples. They discussed price. The margin was a bit thinner than Theresa would have liked, but she calculated that she could make enough to double her profits after she deducted all out-of-pocket expenses. They agreed upon ordering procedures, lead times and delivery schedules. They struck a deal.

Then it hit her—something she should have realized from the first phone call. She could not possibly make all of the salsa herself. There just weren't enough hours in the day or days in the week. She simply couldn't do it by herself. Theresa was going to have to hire her first employee. She sat with her head in her hands. No one could make salsa the way she did. That was the point. That's why she went into business, because she made salsa better than anyone else did. So, how could she hire someone to make salsa and then put her name on it? Would this even be ethical? How could it be Theresa's Extra Special Salsa if someone else made it? Giving up even a part of the responsibility for making the salsa was a deeply personal thing. Theresa found it to be difficult.

Growth is one of the results of success. A business owner can certainly make a decision not to grow a business beyond a certain size. Still, most companies will reach the point where they have to hire the first employee. Theresa had come to that junction. To fulfill the contract she was about to sign, she would have to hire an employee. She was going to have to let go to grow. It is always a challenge to know when to hire the first employees. In addition to being an emotional issue, it's a financial commitment. Hiring your first employee can double your people costs. Fortunately, there are options. For example, the first employees can be part-time. Theresa decided that she would hire a person to work twenty-five hours per week.

It's a huge temptation for the new entrepreneur to hire friends and family. It's a comfortable thing to do. After all, you know the people you are hiring. However, this often-trod path is risky at best. First, it is always better to hire the most qualified person. That may be a friend **Business owners will have to let go to grow. Success will mean delegating the primary work of the business to others.** or family member, but not likely. Second, if things "go south," and they very often do, it can be very difficult to dismiss a family member. It makes Thanksgiving dinner less pleasant. "Sorry I had to fire you Cousin Bill, would you please pass the turkey?" Hiring is critical. Accordingly, we will cover this subject in much more detail in Chapter 6, "Getting the Right Workers in the Right Jobs."

After much thought, Theresa decided that her new hire should be someone with whom she did not have a personal relationship. She also decided this person would be a production employee. For sure, the new hire would help with anything needed, but the primary responsibility would be making salsa. That's really where she needed help. After a lot of thought, Theresa decided that perhaps the new employee could make salsa almost as good as hers, if they followed a very exact recipe.

Theresa had never used a recipe. Oh, she put the same ingredients into every batch, but it was second nature for her. She didn't need to measure. No, the important thing was taste. Like most good chefs, Theresa added salt until the salsa tasted right. To get just the right amount of jalapeño in the mix, she tasted it. Friends had asked Theresa for her recipe many times. She always said, "I will be happy to tell you what's in it, but I can't tell you how much of each ingredient to use. I'm afraid I don't know. I just keep putting more in until it tastes right." It dawned on Theresa that this is one of the reasons that no one else could make salsa as well as she did.

She thought that she would still be able to taste every batch. She could be the quality control person. Still, she needed to tell her new employee exactly how to make the salsa. So, one Sunday afternoon, Theresa's "day off," she went into her kitchen and started making salsa in a very different way. She measured. Most measures were by volume, some by weight. She measured every ingredient carefully. By midnight, Theresa had completed her fourth batch. She thought she had the exact recipe. Actually, it was more detailed than a typical recipe from a cookbook. Theresa specified every step in the process. She detailed which knives, cutting boards and pans to use and in what order. She laid out procedures and specifications for cutting the vegetables and stirring the ingredients.

Without knowing it, Theresa was creating process documentation. This would allow her to communicate to her new employee exactly how she wanted things done. Micro businesses and small businesses can often get by without this formality. The principal can personally supervise every step in the process. Verbal direction can be enough. The principal provides personal instruction to every new employee on how to perform every step in the process. She or he watches the new employee like a hawk until repeated competency is demonstrated. But actually, it's not a bad idea to start documenting processes when the business is in its infancy as Theresa did. It's just easier and more useful to do at an early stage. By the time a business reaches midsize, documented processes become necessary. (We will cover this topic in more detail in a later chapter.)

Remember, when launching a new enterprise, the principal will need to do the primary work of the business. Accordingly, it's critical that the principal have the skill set and the desire to do this work. Being able and willing to do the primary work of the business, while necessary is not sufficient. It's equally important to remember that there is more to running a business than doing its primary work. The owner will need to perform many ancillary functions and it is critical that they do them well. Start a company because you want to run a business, not because you want to do the primary work of the business. Launching a company simply to allow yourself to do the primary work of the business is probably not advisable. You will be setting yourself up to do a lot of other work as well. Finally, it is important to realize that if you wish to grow your enterprise, at some point, you will have to let go of doing the primary work of the business.

Lessons for Successful Growth

If you are contemplating starting a business, make sure that you:

- Possess the requisite skills and the desire to do the primary work of the business

- Recognize the need to perform ancillary functions

- Realize that growth means you will have to let go of doing the primary work of the business at some point

4: Making Tactical Decisions

Kara and Frank had been colleagues for more than a year. They caught the bus at the same stop in the morning. They rode to work together, worked on the same production floor and at the end of the day took the same bus home.

One afternoon Kara made an appointment with Larry, the Vice President of Manufacturing. Larry was her boss's boss's boss. He sat three levels above her in the organization. She reported that Frank, her fellow production worker, had been harassing her both on the bus and on the production floor. Kara claimed that he had been making comments of a sexual nature. She found Frank's comments disgusting and wanted them to stop—now! Larry promised to take care of the matter.

Within minutes of Kara leaving, Larry called Frank into his office. Larry had a simple message for Frank, "I am firing you for sexual harassment." Frank was astonished and denied any wrongdoing. He tried to explain. Larry interrupted Frank's explanation. He was having none of it. Frank was done. He terminated him on the spot.

Larry's decision turned out to be a costly one. In a subsequent hearing, the arbitrator found that the company failed to conduct a proper investigation. As in many of these types of situations, the truth was never fully known. That wasn't actually the point. The point was that Larry hadn't tried to discover the truth. He had not given Frank a chance to rebut the accusation. He didn't interview any witnesses. He didn't insist on getting specific events or times from Kara. Instead, he made a decision without conducting a proper investigation. Within a few weeks, the company terminated

Larry, in part because of the aftermath of his hasty firing of Frank.

Larry recognized the accusation of sexual harassment to be a serious problem. He was right. He also felt compelled to respond immediately. This assessment was incorrect. While Larry needed to address the complaint, there was time to conduct a proper investigation and to hear both sides of the story. His improper assessment of the situation and his knee-jerk reaction caused him to make a bad tactical decision. It cost the company money, and both Frank and Larry lost their jobs.

Obviously, making decisions—good tactical decisions—is one of the most important activities for micro and small business owners. But, how does one ensure good tactical decisions are being made? While nothing can guarantee that every decision will be the right one, you can enhance the quality of tactical decisions by recognizing the nature of the decision.

Two factors are critical: importance and urgency. We define an important decision as one that has the potential to have a significant impact on the business or on a person's life. For example, a decision to terminate a long-term employee is usually an important decision because it will have a significant impact on the employee. An urgent decision is one that you must make immediately; for whatever set of reasons, there is no time for further consideration. When the building is on fire, the decisions regarding what to do are urgent. If you consider these two dimensions together, the result is the four-box matrix shown below.

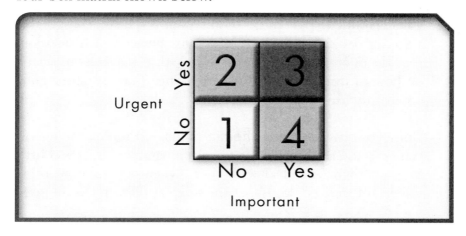

In this example, Larry incorrectly assessed the situation to be both important and urgent (quadrant 3). It was important, but not urgent (quadrant 4). Larry's incorrect assessment caused him to make a decision without proper investigation. This led to the mistake and the unfortunate consequences for all involved. In this chapter, we will consider each of the four quadrants and the resulting implications for tactical decision-making.

Quadrant 1 – Neither Important nor Urgent

These decisions do not have significant consequences. You can delay them, if necessary. They don't deserve much of your time and we won't spend much time on them either. The only real risk here is that a principal spends too much valuable time and resources on these decisions when there are other, more important issues that need attention. Don't spend ten dollars to analyze a fifty-cent decision.

1. **Consider taking no action** – Sometimes when a decision is neither urgent nor important, you don't need to do anything. If you simply ignore the situation, it will resolve itself without your spending any time or effort. A good question to ask before investing time in addressing a quadrant 1 issue is, "What will happen if I do nothing?" Depending on the answer to that question, the issue may be resolved.

2. **Delegate to others** – If there are other employees in the business, these are good decisions to delegate. The risk is low. There is time to pass them off and even if the employee makes a wrong decision, there is little consequence. Such decisions provide an opportunity for the principal to coach subordinates on how to think about decision-making. They can be a good opportunity to develop your staff.

3. **Delay decisions to less hectic times** – If there is no opportunity to use these decisions to develop employees, spend little time on them and deal with them when you have no other important work to do. Resist the temptation to focus on items

that you can check off your "To Do" list quickly when there are other more important and urgent decisions that need attention. In the hierarchy of priorities, decisions that are neither important nor urgent should rank at the bottom.

4. **Beware of morphing** – The only caution is to be aware that decisions can morph over time. A decision that is neither important nor urgent at one point may become either urgent, important, or both at a later date. For example, consider the decision regarding whether or not to hire a college student as a summer intern. In January, this may be neither important nor urgent. By April, it still might not be important, but it is certainly urgent. If you don't make a decision quickly, there may be no qualified students left to hire.

Neither Important nor Urgent
- **Consider taking no action**
- **Delegate to others**
- **Delay decisions to less hectic times**
- **Beware of morphing**

Quadrant 2 – Urgent but not Important

Many tactical decisions need your attention in the short term. These decisions are urgent. At the same time, these decisions may not be of major consequence, and accordingly, are unimportant. Therefore, it is important to choose a direction quickly, but not spend too much time, effort or money analyzing the decision.

1. **Don't over analyze** – Because these decisions are not important, going through a lengthy process to make the decision simply doesn't make any sense. In some outrageous cases the cost of the time spent analyzing a decision can exceed the cost of making a wrong decision. In such instances, you would be better off simply flipping a coin to decide the issue. Don't waste time analyzing decisions that have little or no consequence. A useful way to short circuit the process is to use principles to guide your decisions.

2. **Use principles** – A newly minted Harvard MBA joined McKinsey & Company, a venerable old management-consulting firm. Early in his career, the recent graduate took a business trip to New York City. While staying at the Berkshire Place Hotel just across Madison Avenue from the firm's New York office, he purchased a copy of the *Wall Street Journal* to read while enjoying his breakfast. When it came time to fill out his expense report, he was unsure about how to handle this admittedly small expense. Should he charge it to his client or absorb it himself?

Wanting to do the right thing, he asked the partner responsible for the engagement how to proceed. He was surprised that the partner didn't answer his question directly. Rather, he asked, "Have you met Marvin Bower?" The new associate had met Marvin. He was the patriarch of the firm. He also knew that Marvin Bower had the highest ethical standards. The partner responded, "If you would be comfortable explaining to Marvin that you spent your client's money this way, then go ahead and expense it. If explaining your rationale for expensing the item would make you uncomfortable, then absorb the expense yourself." The young associate never again needed to ask about what items to expense. He had a principle to guide his decisions. By the way, he did not claim the cost of the newspaper on his expense report.

This simple principle saved McKinsey the trouble of having to document what associates could and could not expense. In reality, it's almost impossible to specify item-by-item what is acceptable to expense. You will inevitably leave something off the list. There will always be grey areas. The fact is that the cost of a newspaper, a cab ride, or a lunch is inconsequential when compared to McKinsey's fees. The decision regarding which of these items to expense may have been urgent because expense reports were due, but it was certainly not important. The guiding principle was a simple, inexpensive and quick way to provide necessary direction.

Bernard Robinson, the owner of Networking Technologies and Support, Inc. (NTS), a company that provides IT networking support services explained what he called the two-hour rule. When technicians are in the field, they often have to make a decision regarding when to stop trying to solve a problem and ask for help. Bernard tells his technicians, "If you can't solve the problem within two hours, ET phone home. Don't continue to struggle with the issue; get help from your supervisor." This simple principle makes it easy for his technicians to know when to cut their losses and seek advice.

A company we worked with decided that their guiding principle was to be the easiest company in the industry with which to do business. The company built its strategy on this very clear and straightforward foundation. It provided employees with an acid test for decision-making: What will make things easier for our customers?

For years, business consultants have advised companies to "Stick to the knitting." Learn to do one thing really well and repeat it again and again. The hedgehog has become a popular metaphor for the same concept. To defend itself from would-be predators, the hedgehog only knows how to do one thing, and that is to curl up in a ball with its sharp spines pointed outward. It's simple, it's boring, it's unimaginative, and it works... every time! Once a business identifies its hedgehog concept, it can serve as the underpinnings of every decision in the company. This is particularly useful when making urgent, but unimportant decisions.

The business described above, which chose as its guiding principle "to become the easiest company in their industry with which to do business," empowered its employees to act. When faced with a decision about whether or not to accept a questionable return, product managers knew to err on the side of making things easier for the customer.

On occasion customers requested the shipment of a partial order rather than waiting for the entire order to be available.

When this occurred, the warehouse manager knew to go ahead with the partial shipment even though it would mean extra shipping expenses. Certainly, the company shouldn't and didn't capitulate in every case. Still, if the decision was less than completely clear, employees knew how to make the judgment.

3. **Listen to your gut** – Researchers have explored the anatomy of rapid cognition. These are snap judgments that bubble up from our unconscious self, decisions made in a moment without contemplation. They have concluded, in part, that experts with years of experience in a field can often make very good decisions extremely quickly, although often they can't explain why they reached a particular conclusion. However, even if these experts can't provide a rationale for their conclusions, when the enterprise needs to make a quick decision, it can still benefit from their rapid judgment.

This theory resonates with many executives. A respected manager shared that when decisions are urgent but not important, he goes with his gut. He explained that over the years he has learned his decision-making instincts are actually quite good. Therefore, most of the time, following his gut feeling leads to the proper decision. Even if the decision turns out to be a bad one, the cost is low.

Urgent but not Important
- **Don't over analyze**
- **Use principles**
- **Listen to your gut**

Further, he explained that going against his instincts and then finding that it was a poor decision really angers him. "I knew it! I knew that was a bad decision!" is an unhappy refrain. By following his gut feel, even if the decision turns out to be a poor one, he has the satisfaction of knowing that he didn't waste time on an unimportant decision and he did what he thought was right.

Obviously, using principles and following your gut won't ensure that every decision is a correct one. But, these guidelines will go a long way toward helping streamline decision making when timeliness is important and the consequences are minimal.

Quadrant 3 – Both Important and Urgent

You should avoid this quadrant. Important decisions, made without time for appropriate analysis and contemplation, are often suboptimal. Great insight can sometimes come in a blink, but for decisions of great importance, it's best if this initial feeling is but one piece of information that feeds into the decision.

1. **Prevent morphing** – Decisions often morph into this quadrant. Don't let that happen. A decision that is important but not urgent, if ignored long enough, can become urgent. Consider the case of a new product launch. The company has purchased advertising space months in advance for the marketing campaign. You have planned for the long lead times needed to get the raw material in stock. You have also planned for manufacturing capacity so that machine time and production workers are available to make the initial runs of the new product.

   Still, months before production has to start, some significant design decisions remain. These decisions are very important because they could determine the success or failure of the launch. Nevertheless, the decisions aren't urgent. There's still plenty of time for focus groups, surveys and market research to provide input into these critical decisions.

   However, if you ignore the design decisions long enough, they will become urgent. The advertising is going out. Production has to start. You must finalize the design. Now, because the decision is urgent, there is no time for the analytic work needed to aid in making the determination. Be sure to make important decisions in a timely manner so that they don't morph into situations that are both important and urgent.

2. **Beware of false urgency** – When a decision is important, resist false urgency. One tactic used by high-pressure salespeople is to fabricate an urgent situation. We've all seen the signs, "Once in a lifetime opportunity," "Good for today only." Don't believe it, and don't be pressured into untimely decisions. Most opportunities will come around again. Most successful automobile salespersons will ask you, "What do I need to do to get you behind the wheel of this car before you leave the lot today?" They want you to buy now. Giving you time to contemplate your decision is a bad thing from their prospective. Don't let false deadlines and high-pressure tactics cause you to make a decision that you may regret later.

   A good question to ask when facing possible fabricated urgency is, "What's the worst thing that could happen if I take more time to make this decision?" In many cases the consequences of postponing action are small, but the cost of a hasty decision that turns out to be a poor one may be considerable. Take the time to make a well-thought-out decision.

3. **Reduce urgency** – If the urgency is real, explore opportunities to buy time. Are there ways to lessen the urgency? For most, taxes are important. If left unattended, by April 15, they will also have become urgent. Of course, there is an alternative. If you need more time to do a proper job of completing the tax forms, you can pay the taxes you think you will owe and file an extension. The extension doesn't change the taxes you will have to pay. The importance is still there, but you have reduced the urgency. There are often ways to mitigate the urgency of an important decision. It's worth exploring those possibilities. Don't get forced into a hasty decision that may be suboptimal.

4. **Keep options open** – If there are no opportunities to delay the decision, consider options that will allow the most flexibility in the future. For example, the contractor says he needs a decision right now regarding the parking lot of the new plant. Will it be gravel or asphalt? Failure to make the call now will jeopardize the timely opening of the facility, which could cost

hundreds of thousands of dollars. The gravel option is less expensive, but will require more maintenance. You'd like more time to talk to other plant managers to see what their experiences have been. Unfortunately, there is no time for that right now. You need to make a decision.

If you choose asphalt, the money is spent. You can't easily change the decision. If you choose gravel, options remain. If you put gravel down first, you can apply asphalt later. The total cost of doing this is only marginally more than using asphalt in the first place. In this situation, it probably makes sense to go with gravel first, because the option to use asphalt remains. This will provide the time to complete the desired research before committing to the more expensive option. When forced to make an important decision in a timeframe that does not allow for the desired analysis, consider choosing options that allow flexibility in the future.

5. **Consult experts** – Sometimes the urgency is real, you can't reduce it, and options to maintain flexibility are limited. In such situations, you must make an important decision without the time for the desired research, analysis and contemplation. The decision maker must decide as though it were a quadrant 2 issue: urgent, but not important. In such cases, if possible, seek the council of experts. These are the people who are the most likely to have immediate insight as to the correct direction to proceed. Their trained subconscious can utilize rapid cognition to reach a good decision.

While consulting experts is a good course of action when faced with a decision that is both urgent and important, be cautious about abdicating the responsibility for making critical decisions to anyone. Remember, no one will care about your business as much as you do. Talk to experts. Consider their opinions. More importantly, understand why they think the things they do and incorporate their ideas into your own decision-making process. Remember, the decision is yours, and you have to own it. You are the one who will have to live with the consequences—good or bad.

If there is not even time to consult an expert, follow a guiding principle—look to the hedgehog for guidance. If this fails too because there is no applicable guiding principle, the manager will have to go with his or her gut. This is not the best way to make important decisions, but when all other avenues are blocked, there is no choice.

Quadrant 4 – Important but not Urgent

To achieve outstanding performance over time, a business must have a high success rate when making decisions that are important but not urgent. Because the decisions are important, by definition, getting good results matters a lot. Because they are not urgent, there is time to respond appropriately. In our experience, five things will lead to better decisions:

1. Identify and address the right problem
2. Have the right mindset
3. Utilize appropriate analytical tools
4. Seek the counsel of experts
5. Live with your decision before executing

This is the quadrant where successful companies have a high batting average. You've got time on your side. Take advantage of it.

1. **Identify and address the right problem** – High energy physicists grapple with some of the most complex problems known to mankind. They struggle with questions about the very nature of time, space, matter and its relationship to energy—things that most of us can't begin to comprehend. Bill Hesse was among the most highly respected practitioners in this field. He shared with us that solving extremely difficult problems is not about answering one really tough question. Rather, solving complex problems requires asking a series of questions that are relatively easy to answer. The answers to these more straightforward questions then lead you to the solution of the more complicated issue.

When faced with a problem that is important but not urgent, make sure that you are focusing on the correct problem. Take complex issues and break them down into a series of questions that are easier to answer.

For example, we worked with a company that was considering launching a new product line. The CEO was enamored with the technology. Further, this new technology was, without question, going to cannibalize a significant portion of the existing business. If the company didn't capitalize on this opportunity, others would. Not launching the new product line could potentially leave the company standing by itself in the cold.

Pursuing the new technology meant taking the company in an entirely new direction, a bold strategic decision that would set the course for decades. It was an exciting move. The CEO decided to go for it. Was it a good idea to go in this direction? Perhaps it was hard to tell at the time. Yet, if he had asked the right series of simple questions, the answer would have been a bit clearer. Consider these questions and their answers:

> Q: What is the cost of developing the technology and can we afford it?

> A: The technology will cost tens of millions of dollars to develop. The company could possibly afford to develop the products, but there is no room for a false step. One wrong move and it could be game over. It's a "bet the company" decision.

> Q: Does the company have the expertise to manufacture the new technology?

> A: No, the company has expertise in stamping and plating metal parts that it then inserts into molded plastic housings. The new technology requires software and firmware expertise. The company will need to acquire new skills.

Q: Does the company's sales force have the expertise to sell the new technology?

A: No, the sales force currently lacks the technical expertise to sell the new technology. Either the company will need to replace its sales force or provide extensive training. Morphing the sales force will likely be a complex process that will require elements of both strategies described above.

Q: Who will the competitors be in this new technology?

A: The competitors will be companies such as Allen Bradley, Honeywell, Siemens and ABB. Not only do these companies have much deeper pockets that will enable them to fund the development, but they are also our biggest customers. To win in this new technology, we will have to compete with, and win against, our best customers who are the giants of the industry and who are committed to this direction. Competing against your customers is not usually a winning strategy.

Q: Are there other options for how the company can compete?

A: Yes, the company could offer to provide the plastic housings and electronic components that their competitors will need, (the company does have the expertise to deliver these required elements). Alternatively, the company could look for other products it could manufacture with its existing capabilities and sell with its existing sales force. For example, the company might have moved into selling electrical sensors and switches.

The answers to these questions make the decision to pursue the new technology look a bit more like a suicide mission than a bold new direction. Unfortunately, the CEO did not ask these questions before making his decision. How did it turn out? Not well. The company poured tens of millions of dollars into the development of the new technology, but never came up with a marketable product. Their better-heeled competitors captured the new market. The CEO was fired. The company had to sell off significant portions of its business to stay afloat. While admittedly this decision was more strategic than tactical, it illustrates the value of asking the right questions before making an important decision.

Closely akin to asking the right questions is a technique called reframing. It involves looking at a problem from a different perspective. For example, a woman came to us who ran an organization which helped migrant workers find non-agricultural work. She wanted help figuring out how to dismiss a 25-year employee in the least disruptive way possible. The employee had been effective in the early days and with her experience was a valuable asset. Unfortunately, over the years the clientele had become predominantly Spanish speaking. The long-term employee, who did not speak Spanish, lost effectiveness because she couldn't communicate with the clientele.

We chose to focus on reframing the problem rather than on terminating the employee. How could the long-term employee develop the ability to communicate effectively with the clientele? Learning Spanish at an acceptable level would take too long and the employee was near retirement age. We sought other options. Suppose the organization hired one of the migrant workers, who is fluent in both Spanish and English, as a translator. This would solve the communication issue. It would further the objective of the organization because it would help one more migrant worker to find non-agricultural employment. Perhaps best of all, the translator might be trained to take over the job when the long-term employee retired in a few years.

Originally, the organization saw the problem as, "How can we dismiss a long-term employee in the least disruptive way?" We reframed it to be, "How can we help the long-term employee to communicate effectively with the clientele?" Admittedly getting to this point took some time and was an iterative process. However, at the end of the process we had a better outcome. The result was a win for the employee, the organization, and the migrant worker hired as a translator. Reframing is a particularly powerful tool to use in group problem-solving sessions because group members build on each other's ideas.

When faced with a problem, you should concentrate on addressing the root cause. In today's fast-paced business environment, it is easy to operate in reactive rather than proactive mode. However, when we don't stop to ask "Why" and only solve the immediate issue or the surface problem, we are likely to see the situation again.

A broker/dealer with which we worked occasionally had issues with financial wire transmissions. It seemed that every few weeks a wire transfer would fail to go through. When this occurred, the expectant recipient would register a complaint. The broker/dealer would verify that the wire should have, but did not go through, at which point a customer service person would "force" the transfer. This solved the problem for the customer and the overworked staff moved on to other challenges.

When the company told us about the issue, we asked the simple question, "Why did the wire transfer fail in the first place?" We continued to ask why until we arrived at the root of the problem. It turned out that in writing the software for the wire transfer screen, the field used to enter the transfer number had been limited to only a certain number of characters. The program allowed the processor to enter all the characters, but then it ignored those characters that were beyond its limit. The number of characters allowed more than 97 percent of all wires to transfer satisfactorily. However, one special type of wire required that the processor enter a few additional characters to complete the transaction. The IT department easily fixed the issue and the broker/dealer ceased to have issues with wire transmissions.

When a problem occurs, correcting the immediate issue is important. You must make things right for the customer.

However, making things right for the customer is, by itself, often not sufficient. Once you address the situation at hand, it is critical to ask, why did the problem occur in the first place and what should you do to ensure that it never happens again? Proactively getting to the root of the problem will keep it from recurring. It may take a bit of extra effort in the short-term, but will save a lot of time and aggravation in the long run.

The first step in making decisions that are important but not urgent is to ensure that you have identified the right problem. Tackle a series of simple and clear questions rather than one that is complex and opaque. Try reframing problems to reach a creative win-win solution. Finally, make sure that you get to the root cause and are not simply addressing surface issues.

2. **Have the right mindset** — A wise father taught his child not to make emotional, knee-jerk decisions. When the child did something wrong, the father would often send her to her room while he contemplated his course of action. After some time, the wise father would call the child out of her room and administer the punishment. Years later, he explained that when he sent his daughter to her room, it was because he was angry. He didn't want to punish the child while he was in that state of mind. The break gave him time to ask himself, "What do I need to do to correct my daughter's behavior? How can I help her grow from this experience?"

Later, the wise father taught his daughter to apply this rule more generally. When something really infuriating happens, he advised to stop and ask two questions before reacting: (1) What do I want to happen next? (2) What do I have to do to maximize the probability that that occurs?

Something has transpired that you really don't like. What do you want to happen next? The answer is not revenge. That may make you feel better for a moment, but it's not really what you want to happen. For example, suppose you have just lost a big customer. You think the selection process was unfair. You have served the customer well for years. There was no reason for you to lose the account. Then you find out that the new sales rep of a competitor is dating the owner's administrative assistant. You're sure that she biased the owner's judgment against you. What do you want to happen next?

Slugging someone may feel good, but you'll probably be arrested. That'll just make matters worse. You will still have lost the customer and you'll be in jail. You may wish that you hadn't lost the customer, but that's denying reality. The customer is gone and you're not going to get them back, at least not right now. The real answer is probably that you want to replace the lost revenue, maybe even with a more profitable account.

This leads to the second question. What do you have to do to maximize the probability that this happens? In our experience, it's amazing how seldom the answer to this second question is to give someone a piece of your mind. The appropriate response is usually much more productive than this. Once you have the answers to these two questions clearly in your mind, get on with it.

What the wise father was teaching his child is that before you make an important decision, be sure you are in the right mindset. Take the emotion out of the decision. You shouldn't make important decisions in anger. You should also avoid making decisions in a state of irrational exuberance. Rather, important decisions should be well-thought-out and appropriate responses to each situation.

While it's true that you should not make important decisions while in an emotional state, you must face reality. As mentioned earlier, confronting the brutal facts leads to good decisions. Making good decisions requires an objective assessment of the situation. The CEO described above, who led his midsize business into battle against ABB, Honeywell, Allen Bradley and Siemens refused to confront the reality of his situation. This led him to fight a battle that he had little to no chance of winning. There's a fine line between bravery and stupidity. Decision makers who fail to confront the reality of their situations have crossed that line and they will inevitably pay the price.

Even after you have quelled the emotion of the moment and have confronted the brutal facts, it's important that you recognize that we filter all decisions through our value system. This is normal and natural. However, understanding how your value system influences your decisions can help you to make better decisions. We've identified three value modes used in decision-making:

Pragmatic – People who have a pragmatic value mode process decisions based on achieving a goal. A particular decision is either right because it moves us toward our goal or wrong because it does not. This is a value mode based on logic. Pragmatic people make bottom-line decisions without letting personal feelings influence them. They pay little attention to how their decisions affect others. They will also resist the urge to protect themselves from unpleasant or painful decisions, charging ahead for the good of the organization at all costs. In extreme cases, they may even put aside ethics to achieve the goal.

We worked with one senior executive who recommended that his organization merge with another similarly sized company knowing that he was likely to lose his job in the process. Although the parent company would probably not have gone through with the merger without the strong recommendation of this senior executive, he was able to put the good of the company over his personal interests. As it turned out, part of the merger deal included the president from the incoming organization taking the senior executive's position in the newly merged company. The senior executive lost his job. When asked how he was able to make this challenging decision, he would only say that it was the "right" thing to do. It was best for the shareholders.

Ethical/Moral – People who function in the ethical/ moral mode work from a feeling perspective. For them it's a matter of good versus evil, or right versus wrong. They tend to be highly empathetic and ask questions having to do with the impact that decisions will have on people or other issues concerning individual values (e.g., wildlife, religion, or the environment).

During the recession of 2008-2010, we interviewed a small business owner who refused to lay off his employees or cut their salaries even though his company was losing money each month. He thought of his employees as family and could not bring himself to let any of them go or reduce their income. He knew that many of them lived from paycheck to paycheck. Instead, he cut back his own pay, telling us that he had more discretionary income than his staff.

Hedonistic – Individuals with a predilection for the hedonistic value mode strive to increase pleasure and reduce pain. They will put off painful decisions as long as possible and often procrastinate over doing what they know they need to. In addition, people working from this mode will sometimes justify poor decisions and/or behaviors if the results bring them joy.

We worked with a Vice President of Sales for a midsized electronics firm who tolerated an underperforming sales-person for several years rather than confront the employee about his failure to meet sales targets. The VP's desire to be liked and his discomfort with direct confrontation meant decreased revenue in the highly valued territory. The VP eventually left the firm. The new VP of Sales terminated the underperforming salesperson.

All three modes can produce good business decisions. However, thinking about a decision from each of the value modes will help you consider possibilities that may not occur to you if you remain in a single mode.

Consider the case of this senior executive. When asked what decision he regretted most in his career, he replied, "Not firing Judy." More than 15 years after the event, this executive still smarted over not terminating his administrative assistant when he found her cheating on her vacation time.

Judy had taken an extra week of vacation, one day at a time, which she had not reported to the payroll department. The executive had kept careful records regarding Judy's attendance in his own calendar. At the end of the year; he totaled things up and noted the discrepancy. When confronted, Judy stated that the company owed her the extra time off because she occasionally worked more than forty hours in a week and had not received overtime compensation. She had decided that she would take "comp time" instead.

While wage and hour laws would not have allowed Judy to take comp time in lieu of overtime pay, what ensued was a protracted debate as to her classification—exempt vs. non-exempt. The company's attorneys eventually determined that the classification was correct. The administration assistant was an exempt employee and therefore was not entitled to overtime compensation for the weeks she worked more than forty hours. The executive was right.

He had a gut feeling his assistant had knowingly cheated the system. While he acknowledged he still had some doubt, he was fairly certain he had caught her in a lie. He decided to cut her a break. Unfortunately, it was too late. The experience had soured the relationship between them. Although she feigned loyalty, she began to undermine the executive. Ultimately, she even wrote to the Board of Directors alleging misconduct on the executive's part. She was at least partially successful in sabotaging his engagement with that company.

The executive, in an attempt to be "more than fair," decided to give Judy a second chance. He was operating in the ethical/moral mode. Had he considered the decision from a pragmatic perspective, he would likely have terminated her and avoided a lot of unnecessary controversy. As it turned out, his decision had devastating results—proving the axiom that no good deed goes unpunished.

Ultimately, you'll make the decision that you think is most appropriate. However, in the long run you will make better decisions if you consider more than one point of view.

3. **Utilize appropriate analytic tools** – For decisions that are important but not urgent, it is sometimes helpful to use decision-making tools. There is time to apply the tools and the cost of doing so is justified by the magnitude of the decision. Here's a brief overview of three types of analytic tools:

  o Divergent Tools

  o Convergent Tools

  o Problem-Solving Tools

Divergent tools are those that help you to identify possibilities. They don't typically lead directly to a solution of the problem or make the decision for you. In fact, they don't even limit the field of possible answers. They do exactly the opposite. They expand the range of possibilities and help you to ensure that you haven't overlooked opportunities.

The most basic of divergent tools is a brainstorming session. This generally consists of a small group of people trying to generate possible solutions to an agreed upon problem. The rules of engagement for such meetings usually include a prohibition against speaking negatively about another participant's contribution. At this stage in the process, the point is not to arrive at an answer, but to make sure that you consider all the possibilities. Even a wild idea that might never work could spark a more practical thought in another participant.

Another divergent tool that has gained great popularity as a part of quality improvement programs is a technique called Fishboning (also known as an Ishikawa diagram or a

Cause-and-Effect diagram). This tool facilitates the identification of the potential causes of a specific problem.

There are a large number of popular business frameworks in the divergent tools category such as the McKinsey Seven S model and Michael Porter's Five Forces model. Other models include those often seen in business school marketing classes such as the four Ps (price, product, promotion and place) or the four Cs (company, consumer, competition, and channel). The point is that there are a large number of divergent analytic tools, far too many to describe here.

The primary purpose of these tools is to help people to be exhaustive in their thinking about a particular problem. They are unlikely to lead you to definitive answers in and of themselves, but they will help to ensure that you don't inadvertently ignore big pieces of the puzzle in developing your solution to the overall problem.

Convergent tools are those that help you narrow down a set of possibilities to the few options that will receive serious consideration. Use these to reduce the number of options and focus on the few that are likely to yield the final solution. This is the exact opposite of the divergent tools discussed above.

It's often appropriate to use one or more divergent tools to identify a comprehensive set of potential solutions, followed by convergent tools to limit those solutions receiving serious focus to a manageable number. Again, the list of convergent tools is extensive. We'll give only a couple of examples.

One of simplest ways of reducing a long list of possible actions is by asking participants to vote for those items that they think are the most important. This can be as simple as posting the possible actions around the room on flip-chart pages. Next, give each participant the same number of sticky dots (say three) and ask them to place one dot beside each of the actions that she or he believes are the most important. The potential solutions receiving the most votes are the ones that will receive further consideration.

Another convergent tool is a Pareto analysis (also known as the 80-20 rule)—twenty percent of the sample will produce 80 percent of the results. For example, if you rank each member of a 50-person sales force from most productive to least productive, it is typical that the top 10 producers (20 percent of the salespeople) will account for 80 percent of the sales. A Pareto analysis allows you to figure out which items are the most important so they can receive focus.

Problem-solving tools help you to identify the best answer. Consider the case of a quality problem in a manufacturing company. Management constructed an Ishikawa diagram to identify numerous possible causes of the quality issue. Voting narrowed the possible solutions to a few, one of which was to buy a new machine. The purchase would require a significant outlay of cash now, but quality improvements would save money every year thereafter for the life of the machinery.

Companies often use Net Present Value (NPV) analysis to assess the value of this type of potential solution. The analysis takes both positive and negative cash flows that happen in the future and discounts them to their current-day value. In theory, if the sum of these discounted cash flows is positive, purchasing the machine is a viable solution. If the NPV is negative, the organization should pursue other options. In reality, what such an analysis does is to help identify what you have to believe to justify the expense.

In the above example, let's assume that a 50-percent reduction in scrap would yield a positive NPV, but a 20-percent reduction would result in a decidedly negative NPV. Since it is difficult to predict a specific scrap reduction rate in advance, you will need to exercise some judgment. Solving real business problems is always about applying judgment. Most often analysis won't give you a definitive answer; rather it will help you understand what judgment you must make.

Charts represent another form of problem-solving tool. They are very useful for presenting data so that the message is clear.

For example, it might be very difficult to discern a trend staring at 10 years of quarterly sales numbers laid out in a column. When the same data is plotted as a line chart, it is easy to see that sales generally increased for the first five years, but then came back down to the original level. You can use different types of charts to illustrate specific points. For example, you can use pie charts to show what percentage of the total each of a series of components represents, or scatter diagrams to show correlation. These days Excel and other similar tools allow analysts to plot an essentially endless number of charts for a given set of data. It is critical to understand what you are trying to show and select your chart type accordingly.

We have not even begun to scratch the surface regarding the analytic tools available to aid in decision-making. When it is appropriate to use analytic tools, there is often benefit to using divergent tools to identify options, convergent tools to limit options to a manageable number, and problem-solving tools to aid in the final assessment of potential solutions.

4. **Seek the counsel of experts** – When considering quadrant 3 decisions, those that are both urgent and important, we suggested that it was a good idea to seek the advice of experts. Experts often have immediate insight into the right path to pursue. We offer the same counsel when considering quadrant 4 decisions, those that are important but not urgent. If experts can help make good decisions on the spur of the moment, they can bring even more value when there is time to consider things more carefully.

We'll address this topic more fully later in the book, but it is appropriate to observe here that too often business owners feel that they have to make decisions by themselves. After all, running the business is their job and they shouldn't need help.

Many business owners began their companies specifically because they were good at doing the primary work of the business. We spoke to the owner of a security business (a provider of burglar alarms, smoke detectors and surveillance equipment). He told us that he started his business because he thought he could do a better job than the man for whom he was working. Similarly, a nurse started a home healthcare business after she was unable to find acceptable care for her dying father. These are only two examples of many. Both make the same point. Many people start businesses because they are experts at the primary work of the business. However, being a good alarm installer or a good nurse does not mean they will know how to run a multimillion-dollar business successfully.

In fact, it's likely that the opposite is true. People aren't born knowing how to run businesses. It's a learned skill. Without the opportunity to receive training and/or be in a position to see first-hand what a well-run business looks like, it is unlikely that they will know how to build an efficient and effective enterprise.

In many cases, entrepreneurs eventually figure out solutions to their problems through trial and error, because they are smart and hardworking. But, why take that chance? If you want to design a house, you could start from scratch. You could learn how thick to make footings by trial and error. You could discover on your own how residential electrical wiring and plumbing work. You could buy a book and piece together the functioning of HVAC systems. Of course, you wouldn't. You'd begin by talking to an architect or a contractor. You'd learn what was possible and what wasn't, what costs too much, what was unsafe and what options were available. You'd take advantage of centuries of accumulated knowledge regarding how to build a house.

Running your business is actually more complex than building a house. When making important decisions, benefit from the success and mistakes of others, build on the accumulated knowledge that already exists, and talk to the experts. By definition, entrepreneurs are people who like to go it alone. They are not afraid to take risks. In this case, resist the temptation. It's just the smart thing to do.

To reiterate a point that we made earlier, considering the advice of wise counselors does not mean abdicating responsibility for decision making to them. The decision is yours. You have to be the one to make it. However, it is wise to incorporate the thinking of experts as you determine how to proceed.

5. **Live with your decision before executing** – After making sure to address the correct problem, ensuring that you are in the right mindset, using appropriate analytic tools and talking to experts, make your decision. Once you have made the decision, assuming there is time, delay for a day or two before announcing your verdict. We're not suggesting indiscriminate hesitation. Rather, we're suggesting that you take this opportunity to listen to your instincts. If during this period, your comfort with the decision increases, execute. However, if doubts arise, it may be useful to revisit the decision-making process. In the final analysis, unnecessary delay is counterproductive. You certainly don't want to wait until a decision that isn't urgent morphs into one that is. Nevertheless, if there is plenty of time, it is often a good idea to take the time to sleep on your decision and listen to your instincts.

Important but not Urgent
- **Identify the right problem**
- **Be in the right mindset**
- **Use analytic tools**
- **Talk to experts**
- **Live with the decision**

Quadrant 4 decisions are important and you have the time to consider them carefully. For your company to be successful, you will need to have a high batting average when making these types of decisions. Nothing can guarantee success, but you will make good decisions more often if you: (1) Take the time to identify the right problem; (2) Ensure that you are in the right mindset; (3) Use the appropriate analytic tools; (4) Seek wise counsel; and (5) Live with your decision for a while before implementing.

Lessons for Successful Growth

Determine into which quadrant of the Tactical Decision Making matrix the decision falls and respond accordingly.

When faced with tactical decisions, it's important to understand the nature of each challenge. Determine if the decision is important and/or urgent. Once that's done, each will fall into one of the four quadrants of the Tactical Decision Making matrix. Respond accordingly.

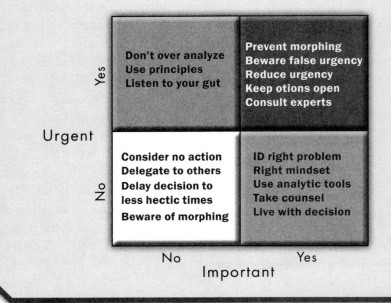

	No	Yes
Yes (Urgent)	Don't over analyze Use principles Listen to your gut	Prevent morphing Beware false urgency Reduce urgency Keep otions open Consult experts
No	Consider no action Delegate to others Delay decision to less hectic times Beware of morphing	ID right problem Right mindset Use analytic tools Take counsel Live with decision

Important

5: Developing a Strategy

John was the guest lecturer for the evening in the capstone course of an MBA program at a well-known university. The title of the course was "Strategic Planning." It was near the end of the semester and students were on the verge of graduation. Most of the men and women in the class held full-time jobs in local businesses and were pursuing their Master's degrees to enhance their careers. The class consisted mainly of first-line managers. All of the students had at least some business experience. John began the class by asking, "So, what is a strategy anyway?" The students responded with blank stares. He repeated the question. Again, silence. John challenged the class, "Come on, you've almost completed a course called 'Strategic Planning,' surely someone here can define strategy for me!"

Finally, one brave soul raised her hand and said, "Porter's Five Forces Model." Not wanting to discourage the class, John said, "Good" (knowing that it wasn't) and he wrote the name of the model on the board. Encouraged, another student chimed in, "BCG Growth Share Matrix." Again, he recorded the comment. During the next two or three minutes, another half-dozen analytic tools made their way onto the board. These included the "McKinsey Seven S Model" and "SWOT Analysis" among others.

> **At its core, business is about *only* two things:**
> * **Figuring out what to do**
> * **Getting it done**

Then John asked, "If I completed all of these analyses for my company, would I have a strategy?" A man sitting in the front row responded sheepishly, "I don't think so, because you still wouldn't have a plan."

Right! At its core, a strategy is just a plan to achieve your business goals. Success in business consists of nothing more than determining what you want to do and then getting it done. First, the principal must develop a plan that will serve as a roadmap for what the business needs to do. Next, and often the more difficult part, get your people to execute the plan.

Please note that developing and ensuring the execution of an appropriate strategy will remain the responsibility of the principal regardless of whether the business is micro, small, or midsize. Therefore, we wrote this chapter without regard for the size of the enterprise. For example, we refer to "senior managers." In a micro or small business the only "senior manager" is the principal. Once the business attains a midsize structure, "senior managers," other than the principal, will exist and the term, therefore, is more relevant.

Figuring Out What to Do

The owners/shareholders of most businesses would like to see the enterprise deliver above-average returns. To have any hope of this, a company must be able to answer one very critical question. What is our competitive advantage? What do we do better than the competition that will allow us to deliver superior returns?

You simply cannot deliver returns that are above average by doing things in an average way. We learned this early in our business careers. A firm can have many different strengths relative to its competitors. However, there are only two basic types of competitive advantage: low cost or differentiation.

> **To achieve above average performance a business must either have a cost structure that is significantly lower than that of its competitors or it must offer a product/service package that is different than that offered by others.**

Low Cost – If a company has a cost structure that is lower than that of its competitors, it can create a sustainable competitive advantage. Walmart is famous for delivering above-average returns using a low cost strategy. A number of years ago, we had the opportunity to visit Walmart's headquarters in Bentonville, Arkansas. The building and its furnishing were extremely austere. Our meeting was not in a plush conference room. Rather, we met in what could best be described as a cubical in the reception area. This was a "no frills" environment. The company obviously kept overhead costs as low as possible.

Further, Walmart is legendary for its aggressive negotiating tactics with its suppliers. It uses its massive volume to buy name-brand products at prices well below what its competitors pay. If they do not receive significantly lower prices than competitors enjoy, the product will not be on the Walmart shelves. Many manufacturers concede on price in order to capture the volume that Walmart can deliver.

The combination of being in a very thin-margin business, with low overhead and low product cost enables Walmart to deliver superior returns while pricing name-brand products below the levels its competitors can offer. Because the company is selling name-brand products, customers perceive that the merchandise they purchase at Walmart is equivalent to what they could buy at more expensive stores. This has enabled the company to increase sales, which further enhances its ability to negotiate low prices with suppliers. It's a virtuous cycle, and it works very well.

While Walmart uses low prices to build market share, you don't have to play this game to get above-market returns. Acme Manufacturing produced the equipment used in a particular sport. There was only one meaningful competitor. Both companies were unionized and had approximately the same cost structure. From the customer's perspective, there was little meaningful difference between the products of the two competitors. Both manufactured high-quality equipment that made playing the sport fun and easy. Further, pricing was similar. The result was that each enjoyed approximately the same share of the market. Both businesses had about $500 million in annual revenue. Each of the companies was profitable, but neither delivered remarkable returns.

Then, an aggressive group of entrepreneurs purchased Acme for approximately $400 million. After negotiations with the union broke down, Acme closed its manufacturing facility in the Midwest. Subsequently, the company opened a new plant in a Sunbelt state, but the company was no longer unionized. Almost overnight, Acme's cost structure was between 20 percent and 25 percent less than that of its only competitor.

Acme could have chosen to reduce its price in an effort to gain market share. Doing so in an industry with good margins would have forced its competitor to reduce prices in order to remain competitive. The result would have been lower overall industry profitability—not a great deal for either competitor. Rather than reducing price, senior management at Acme decided to let the benefit of its newly found competitive advantage flow directly to the bottom line. Brilliant! For the next decade, the owners pulled well in excess of $100 million of cash out of the business each year. The entrepreneurs subsequently sold the business for approximately $1.4 billion. As you can imagine, they became quite wealthy.

Sometimes an organization can create a competitive advantage by targeting a specific segment of the market that it can serve at a fundamentally lower cost. Like most local or regional banks in the 1990s, Signet Bank had a small credit card business. At that time, the interest rate on essentially all credit cards in this country was the same, 18.9 percent. When two ex-consultants, Rich Fairbank and Nigel Morris, took over Signet's credit card operation, they made a very insightful observation about the market. Many low-risk customers were revolving balances at 18.9 percent. Because this segment was low risk, its charge-off rates were substantially lower than the market average. Therefore, the cost to serve this segment was dramatically less than the market average. While an 18.9 percent interest rate may have been necessary to run a profitable credit card operation on average, Signet could serve this one segment very profitably at much lower rates. They had identified an inefficient market, which represented a significant opportunity.

Rich, Nigel and their team invented the balance transfer and targeted the low-risk segment with a lower price product, one that had an interest rate of only 14.9 percent. Even at this lower rate, the low-risk segment was quite profitable because the cost to serve this segment was substantially less than the cost to serve the balance of the market. The result was what Nigel Morris called a "balance vacuum cleaner." Suddenly, the assets of Signet's small credit operation began to grow exponentially. The division was spun off and Capital One was born. While there is certainly more to the story, Rich and Nigel's insight to serve a specific segment at a fundamentally lower cost led directly to the creation of one of the largest financial institutions in the world.

A competitive advantage based on a lower cost structure can be a very powerful thing indeed. It can enable a company to grow its business by pricing below competitors. Walmart has been hugely successful using this strategy. Sometimes the cost advantage is available in only one segment of the market as in the Signet Bank example. That's okay as long as the segment is large enough. Finally, it is important to remember that a cost advantage needn't be exploited by lowering the price. If you can maintain price parity with competitors, a low-cost position will result in higher profits as with Acme Manufacturing.

Differentiation – Sharon Madere is the founder of a company called Premier Pet Products. She started the business in her guest bedroom about twenty years ago. Sharon and her team have developed a series of products that help pet owners to modify the behavior of their dogs in humane ways. Therefore, Premier Pet Products offers differentiated merchandise from that sold by its competitors. For example, perhaps their best-known product is the "Gentle Leader Headcollar." The collar goes around the dog's neck and over its muzzle. The Gentle Leader immediately eliminates pulling on the leash. When you steer the dog's nose, you steer the dog's body. It's a positive, no-pain option for controlling your dog. The collar may not be the least expensive alternative, but it's kinder to the dog.

As you would guess, there is a significant segment of pet owners who are willing to pay a bit more to get a product that doesn't inflict pain on their dog. It turns out that people in this segment will often buy their pet products from a veterinarian or a trainer. Alternatively, they will take advice from vets and trainers regarding the best products to buy. Therefore, Premier Pet Products has worked very hard to educate vets and trainers about their offerings and to establish and maintain outstanding relationships with them. By understanding the needs of one specific segment of the pet products market and identifying how to get their message to this segment, the company has grown from a one-woman micro business to a highly profitable multimillion-dollar enterprise. This product differentiation strategy has worked well for them.

Another company that has used differentiation to build a competitive advantage is Creative. The business offers office furniture, technology, wall systems, and flooring systems. CEO Bob Delille explained, "We offer a differentiated value proposition, one that is unique in our industry. By combining workplace interiors with technology, we create solutions to our clients' problems that competitors can't offer." Many competitors offer workplace interiors. Others offer technology for use in the office. Few, if any, offer both.

It's great to create a differentiated product/service package. Unfortunately, that, by itself, is not enough. In addition, the differentiated product/service package must be more desirable to a specific segment of the market than any alternative. Also, the size of this segment must be large enough to be attractive. For example, you could market a skunk-flavored Popsicle. This would be a differentiated product; nothing remotely resembling such an offering is available in your local supermarket. However, it is highly unlikely that this product would be attractive to a large enough segment of the market to make it an economically viable offering. This is a silly example, but it makes the point that differentiation alone isn't sufficient. You must target the differentiated product/service package to a sufficiently large segment of the market, which values the unique characteristics of the offering.

It's been said that the job of the strategist is to create little monopolies; to identify segments of the market where your company's product/ service package is so differentiated, so uniquely well positioned, that the competition's offering doesn't get serious consideration. In the customer's mind, the competitor's offering may as well not exist. The only real alternative to buying your company's product or service is to do without. When companies differentiate and properly target their products or services in this way, members of the segment are willing to pay significant premiums. Choosing the right market segment in which to compete is critical.

For example, American Express has been able to position their Platinum charge card as a high-end, prestigious product with lots of perks. Platinum cardholders are willing to pay a $450 annual membership fee for the privilege of using this card when they could easily obtain a MasterCard or a Visa for free. People in this segment are willing to pay these premiums because they value what the American Express Platinum card offers. Neither the MasterCard nor the Visa measure up. They just aren't nearly prestigious enough. There can be real value associated with developing a differentiated product/service package and targeting the appropriate market segment.

While market segmentation can be a powerful tool, it isn't a magic wand that always delivers value. We worked with the U.S. operation of a German-owned manufacturer named Weidmüller, Inc. The company sold electrical and electronic components to other manufacturers. In an attempt to grow sales, Weidmüller segmented their market by industry (e.g., chemical, machine tool, package goods, etc.). Sales efforts targeted these industries, but incremental sales growth just didn't happen. The segmentation didn't create additional value. So, why did the segmentation fail? What makes a good market segmentation that will allow companies to target their products and services to customers who will pay a premium for them?

There are two criteria for a segmentation to deliver significant value:

1. Members of the segment must make the buying decision like each other and differently from those not in the segment.

2. Members of the segment must be externally identifiable or they must be willing to self-identify.

In our work with Weidmüller, we identified that the problem with the failed market segmentation described above was simple. The customers in each of the different segments made the buying decision in the same way. The characteristics that were important to customers in the machine tool segment were also important to customers in the chemical and packaged goods segments. Customers in different industry segments did not make the buying decision differently from each other as required by our definition of a good market segment. Instead, they made the buying decision like each other. Therefore, there was no opportunity to differentiate the product/service package to meet the specific needs of one subset of the market. Consequently, segmenting the customer base by industry wasn't helpful.

The key to effectively segmenting a market is to understand how customers make the buying decision. What characteristics of the product/service package are most important to each group of customers?

Ken Aspinall, the CEO of Manchester Industries, a leading paper converter, was discussing how his customers make the buying decision. He observed, "Whoever has the product first gets the order." Ken had identified a segment of the market for which delivery time was the most important factor in the buying decision. Accordingly, Manchester Industries targeted this segment by gearing its processes to deliver quick turnaround. Ken explained that an order received in the morning could ship the same evening and any customer east of the Mississippi would receive it the next day.

Faced with a segmentation that wasn't working, we rethought Weidmüller's approach. We ultimately derived significant value from understanding how customers made the buying decision. It allowed us to tailor their product/service offering to what the target market segment wanted.

> **The key to effectively segmenting a market is to understand how customers make the buying decision.**

In conducting research on how Weidmüller's customers made the buying decision, we discovered that there were some differences of opinion within the company. The sales force insisted that a low price was what customers wanted. That makes sense; they were talking to purchasing agents whose mission was to buy acceptable products at the best prices possible.

Conversely, the design engineers were convinced that customers made the buying decision based on product features. For example, Weidmüller's product scored better on certain force tests than their competitor's products. The design engineers thought this was a key selling point.

The first big insight came from understanding who made the buying decision. It turned out that in a large number of cases, the purchasing agent did not make the buying decision. Instead, it was the design engineer. In this segment of the market, the design engineer would specify only one manufacturer (we'll call this the "Single supplier segment").

The purchasing agent could, of course, try to get another manufacturer approved, but typically, he or she wouldn't go to that trouble. In the single supplier segment, the manufacturer specified by the design engineer was the one bought by the purchasing agent. Being specified was critical. Alternatively, some design engineers would specify multiple suppliers (we'll call this the "Multiple supplier segment"). In this case, price was very important because the purchasing agent would most likely buy from the specified supplier with the lowest price.

It turns out that the design engineers who, in effect, made the buying decision in the single supplier segment didn't care about price or product features. You see, this particular product accounted for a very small percentage of the total cost of the project. Even a significant price difference, of say 10 percent, was inconsequential to the overall cost of the project and therefore to the specifying engineer. Further, as one design engineer told us, "What Weidmüller's product does is very basic; it connects two wires together. Their product does a good job, but so do the products offered by four or five competitors. Product features really aren't important."

We discovered that two things motivated the design engineers. First, they wanted to make sure the product they specified was the right one. Design engineers cannot allow themselves to be responsible for a project that doesn't work. Second, they needed to make the decision about which product to specify quickly. They couldn't spend all day figuring out which product is right for the job. So, in the single supplier segment, the product purchased will be the one that allows design engineers to quickly and accurately determine what to specify. They are willing to pay a premium for this.

This observation led us to the insight that essentially all industrial product catalogs are exactly backwards. If the user knows a part number, she or he can look in the index and find the page that contains the product specifications. Unfortunately, what design engineers know is the specifications. What they want to find is the part number. The only way they can use a typical industrial catalog is by trial and error. Obviously, this isn't a very efficient process.

Faced with this reality, the specifying engineers followed the path of least resistance. By becoming very familiar with the catalog of one manufacturer and specifying only the offerings of that company, the engineer could reduce the time spent searching for the product they wanted. Further, by becoming very familiar with the offerings of one manufacturer they increased the probability that the part they selected would work.

This is a wonderful state of affairs if you are the market leader, because it is difficult for a challenger to take your accounts. This arrangement will perpetuate the status quo. Unfortunately, if you are the challenger trying to grow your market share quickly, this arrangement is a problem. Weidmüller was in the latter position and therefore needed to find a way to change the rules of the game.

Our solution was a computer-based program that allowed the engineers to input what they knew—the specifications. The program then provided the engineer with the appropriate part number. This allowed Weidmüller to use the computer to invert the way individuals found product in a paper-based catalog. Rather than a part number leading to specifications, we designed a program that allowed specifications to lead to a part number. For a design engineer who was not familiar with the company's offerings, this dramatically reduced the search time while also improving the accuracy.

We then took the next step and had software developed that would automatically generate drawings for the specifying engineer using the products that the computer-based program selected. This further simplified the job of the specifying engineer who would willingly follow the path of least resistance.

At this point, the market segmentation looked as though it might be quite useful. We had identified a group of customers that made the buying decision like each other and differently from those in other segments. Further, we had been able to tailor a product/ service offering that was uniquely suited to the needs of that segment. You already know the next question to ask. Is the single supplier segment externally identifiable?

Assuming that differences in the way customers make buying decisions exist, to be useful for market segmentation, the customers in each segment must be externally identifiable. Marketers need to know how to reach the specific segments. Should the company advertise in *Sports Illustrated* or *Cosmopolitan*? While there are, no doubt, some people who read both periodicals, the overlap is not likely large.

Alternatively, the members of a particular segment may be self-identifying. For example, if a man intends to buy a suit, those who walk into Sears versus The Men's Warehouse versus Brooks Brothers are clearly members of different market segments. The marketing for each store would reflect the differences.

Is Weidmüller's single supplier segment externally identifiable? Unfortunately, not immediately—it isn't possible to tell simply by looking at a company's listing in an industrial database whether it is a member of the single supplier segment or the multiple supplier segment.

Fortunately, Weidmüller had hundreds of distributors across the country with literally thousands of salespeople. These salespeople knew which companies were in the single-supplier segment and which were in the multiple-supplier segment. Weidmüller asked the distributor's salespeople to identify companies in the single-supplier segment for them. The company then offered to install its new time-saving software free of charge in any company identified by the sales organization. The only requirement was that the company using the software had to agree to register with Weidmüller. This way, Weidmüller could update the software when necessary. This allowed the company to build a database containing the contact information for customers in the single-supplier segment. This was the best of all worlds. The segment became externally identifiable, but only to Weidmüller, not to its competitors.

Weidmüller's product became the easiest in the industry to specify. They targeted customers in the single-supplier segment that placed a high value on this. The result, sales increased by 50 percent over the course of a couple years. Price pressure declined because they were targeting a segment that wasn't price sensitive. As you would expect, profits soared. The company made more profit over a two-year period than it had made in its prior nineteen years of existence. There is real value to understanding how customers make their buying decisions and targeting your product service offerings to a segment that is willing to pay a premium for it.

Effective market segmentation can be an incredibly valuable tool for increasing profits. However, to gain the benefit, businesses must take the time to understand how customers make buying decisions and what will attract potential customers in their target segment. Although this may sound straightforward, our experience is that the exercise can be complex. The good news is that, when done well, the rewards are more than worth the effort.

When deciding what they want to do, companies have only two ways to create a sustainable competitive advantage. They can choose to pursue a low-cost strategy or one based on a differentiated product/ service package. Walmart sells product that is identical to the offerings of its competitors (brand name merchandise), but because it has a fundamentally lower cost structure, it is able to charge a lower price. Its volume drives profitability. Acme Manufacturing chose not to compete on price, but rather to maintain the status quo in the industry and let the benefit of its low-cost position flow directly to the bottom line. Signet Bank successfully exploited the fundamentally lower cost of serving the low-risk segment of the market.

> **There are two criteria for a market segmentation to deliver significant value. Members of the segment must:**
> - **Make the buying decision like each other and differently from those not in the segment**
> - **Be identifiable**

Weidmüller, Premier Pet Products, American Express and Manchester Industries identified segments of the market that they could serve very profitably with a differentiated product. We helped Weidmüller make their product the easiest in the industry to specify because that was how the customer made the buying decision. Premier Pet Products and American Express identified segments of the market that were prepared to pay a premium for their differentiated products. Manchester Industries provides faster delivery to a segment that values this. In their role as strategists, principals must decide how they want to create a competitive advantage. They can choose to compete based on low cost, product/service differentiation or some combination of the two. The important thing is that they have a clear plan for success.

Getting People to Execute

Once a principal has decided what he or she wants to do, the challenge becomes developing a plan to get people to do it. Our experience suggests that this second step is often the more difficult of the two. To get people to execute the big picture plan, it must be broken down into very specific business goals. All too often, companies fail to do this. In fact, about one-third of the businesses we interviewed reported having no written goals. What frequently happens is that a company goes into business to sell widgets, and sell widgets it does. Without realizing it, senior managers get so busy working *in* the business that they don't get around to working *on* the business.

It's been said that America is the land of opportunity, and in the land of opportunity, people can have anything they want. The trouble is that most Americans don't know what they want because they have never taken the time to write down their goals. The first key to an implementable strategy is to make the time to think through the company's goals in detail.

The renowned philosopher Yogi Berra observed, "If you don't know where you are going, you might wind up someplace else." Goals ensure that everyone in the organization knows where the company is going. However, goals by themselves are not enough. A company must also have a plan to achieve its goals. First, the principal must cascade the goals down throughout the organization. Further, you must establish deadlines and actions step. Next, you must hold individuals accountable for timely delivery of the result. Finally, make sure that the company's human systems are in alignment with the plan.

Establish clear goals – If the goals are clear, everyone can pull in the same direction. However, to set a clear direction, you must write your goals correctly. Poorly written goals won't provide the needed clarity. If you want to develop well-written goals, use the acronym "WHY SMART."

Companies must:
- **Establish clear goals**
- **Develop a plan**
- **Set deadlines and establish clear accountability**
- **Cascade the goals through-out the organization**
- **Ensure human systems work in concert with the plan**

Written – First, you must write down your goals. There is power associated with putting your goals in writing. Many people say, "I know what my goals are. I don't need to write them down." Unfortunately, it doesn't work that way. If goals aren't written down, day-to-day events will overtake them every time. The urgent will trump the important. To be useful, you should write down your goals and review them regularly.

Harmonious – You will inevitably have more than one goal. That's great, but they must be harmonious. The goals shouldn't conflict with each other. For example, if a company sets one goal to be the low-cost producer in the industry and another goal to offer the product with the most bells and whistles, this probably isn't going to work. The goals are not harmonious.

Yours – The senior management team must own the goals. However, ultimately this ownership must be cascaded throughout the company. Employees must be completely committed to getting results. Goals that are forced on the team, say by an outside consultant, but to which the team has not truly bought into, won't work. The probability of success increases exponentially when those who will have to execute against the goals are completely committed to them.

Specific – Vague goals won't be very effective. A goal to "be more successful" could mean many things. Does "being more successful" mean growing sales, increasing profit, improving quality, or something else? If goals aren't specific, they won't provide a clear direction for the company or the employees.

Measurable – Whenever possible, goals should be measurable. You need to know when you have achieved them. "Reducing rework by 25 percent" is a measurable goal. "Improve quality" is not. There are times when it isn't possible to quantify a goal. That's okay, but when possible, goals should be measurable.

Action Oriented – Write your goals so that there are specific actions that can be taken. For example, a goal to "increase profits by 10 percent due to favorable move in exchange rate," is not an action-oriented goal. Exchange rates may well move favorably, but you can't cause it to happen. Favorable exchange rate movement may be a part of your plan, but since there is nothing that you can do that will increase the probability this occurs, it isn't an action-oriented goal. Goals that aren't action oriented are just hopes.

Realistically High – Goals that are very easily attained aren't useful. The reason for setting goals is to drive performance. If you can achieve the goal without significant effort, you probably won't be inspired. Performance will be unaffected. Achieving goals should require effort. At the same time, goals that are set so high that there is no realistic expectation that you can achieve them aren't helpful either. The challenge is to set goals so that employees recognize that with extra effort, they can achieve their goals.

Time and Resource Bound – Goals must be accomplished within a specific timeframe. In addition, you should specify which resources the employees might use. Open-ended goals with no time constraint aren't useful. Planning to grow annual sales by 25 percent is, perhaps, an admirable goal, but you need a time constraint. Without one, it might take 10 years for annual sales to increase by 25 percent. This was probably not the intent of the goal. In the same way, it is fine to set a goal of growing sales by 25 percent this year, but again, you should specify the resource constraints. If you accomplish your goal by tripling the size of the sales force or cutting your prices in half, the cost is likely to exceed the benefit. To ensure that you achieve your goals in a profitable way, they must be time and resource bound.

When a management team develops its goals, asking if each goal meets the requirements of the "WHY SMART" acronym enforces a valuable discipline. When the goals rise to this standard, they will set a clear direction for the organization.

Develop a plan to achieve the goals – Once you have established the "WHY SMART" goals, put an actionable plan in place to achieve them. We worked with one company whose CEO turned around and removed something from his drawer. He presented it as though it were the original of the Gettysburg Address. As he handed it to us he said, "Read this. It's our strategy!"

> **Asking if each goal meets the "WHY SMART" acronym enforces a valuable discipline.**

That evening we studied the document carefully. It contained a plethora of insightful analysis regarding the market, competitors, products, etc. It even spelled out the company's goals. Unfortunately, it did not contain so much as one word about who was going to do what, by when, in order to achieve the goals. While perhaps brilliant analysis, this was most decidedly not a strategy. A strategy requires a detailed plan to achieve the goals. Further, this plan must contain action steps that spell out specifically when each one will be completed.

**Set deadlines for delivery and establish clear account-
ability** – The plan needs to indicate not only what you are
going to do, but also which senior manager is responsible for each
major task and when they will have it completed. It's important
that you assign one, and only one, senior manager responsibility
for each goal. This is called "point accountability" and it's critical
to goal achievement. People are often tempted to assign responsibility for a single goal to multiple people—a team or a taskforce.
Don't fall prey to this temptation. The problem is that when more
than one person is responsible, no one is accountable. It's easy
for each person with his or her name beside a particular goal to
assume that the other person is doing what is necessary to achieve
success. When everyone makes
this assumption, nothing is
done. If there is point accountability, this won't happen. It is
clear who is accountable. It is
fine for the responsible party
to call on others for help in
achieving the goal, but it is
critical that you hold only one
person accountable.

> **Point accountability
> means that one, and
> only one person has
> responsibility for a goal.**

Cascade the goals throughout the organization – For
optimal results, the responsibilities of each senior manager must
be cascaded throughout their respective organizations. In many
cases, the senior manager won't execute the required action items.
Instead, a member of his or her organization will complete the
tasks. Again, point accountability is critical at each level.

Align the goals of everyone in the company with the company
strategy and with each other. Suppose the president of a
company declared to his senior management team, "Our goal
is to increase profits by 30 percent this year, and it is up to
each of you to implement plans to achieve this goal." With
this direction, the VP of Manufacturing surveyed his plant
and decided that the old equipment they were using resulted in
significant inefficiency. Therefore, he decided to replace all of
the old equipment with state-of-the-art machines. He was sure

that this would result in increased productivity, reduced costs and therefore increased profits.

The VP of Human Resources observed that many employees didn't know how to use the old machines effectively. He decided to hire an outside training firm to retrain every manufacturing employee on how to operate the existing equipment. This, he reasoned, would increase productivity, reduce costs and therefore increase profits.

The CFO decided that she would eliminate all non-essential spending to drive costs down and increase profits. Obviously, this company is doomed to fail. While there is alignment between each senior manager's plan and the company goal of increased profits, the managers' plans are not aligned with each other.

Ensure human systems work in concert with the plan – Once you align the goals of every member of the organization with the company's goals and with each other, it is important to ensure that the human systems (e.g., performance management system, compensation system, hiring system, etc.) reinforce goal achievement.

> **Ensure that you align goals with each other and with the overall company strategy.**

For example, one company had a goal to reduce scrap by 15 percent in the current year. Any cost associated with the initiative must be more than justified by the benefit of improved quality. It turns out that the organization could dramatically increase quality, but there was a trade-off. To reduce scrap, the company had to run the machines at a slower speed. This allowed the achievement of the scrap reduction goal. However, it also dropped output by 10 percent. Analysis showed that, economically, slowing the machines was a very good decision for the company. The money that the company would save from reduced scrap more than offset the cost of the lost production.

Human systems must reinforce company goals.

Since the organization pays its production workers a bonus based on productivity with no consideration of quality, it is unlikely that they will be willing to reduce their output in favor of lowered scrap rates. It is decidedly unfair to expect an employee to do something that is in the company's best interest, but that will reduce the employee's income. A company's human systems must be aligned with and reinforce its goals.

Getting people to effectively execute a company's strategy is often more difficult than determining what you want to do. That's why it's important to have a plan for how you will get employees to perform. Following these guidelines will significantly increase the probability of success:

- Develop a set of well-thought-out goals for the organization

- Identify a clear plan to achieve those goals

- Ensure that each step in the plan has a deadline for delivery and a single senior manager who is accountable

- Cascade the goals of each senior manager down throughout their respective organizations so the goals of every employee are aligned with the strategy and with each other

- Ensure that the company's human systems work in concert with these goals

In summary, a strategy is nothing more than a company's plan to achieve its business goals. Developing a successful strategy requires that the principal determine what to do and figure out how to get people to do it. Determining what to do involves deciding how the company will create a sustainable competitive advantage vis-à-vis its competitors. Two paths are available: pursing a low-cost position, or differentiating the company's product/service package so that it is attractive to a significant segment of the market.

Getting people to execute requires developing clear goals and cascading these goals throughout the organization. There must be top to bottom alignment around a clear set of internally consistent organizational goals. Then you must hold your people accountable for delivering against each goal in a timely manner. Developing such a system takes a lot of work, but experience shows that the results are well worth the effort and the cost of failure can be substantial.

Lessons for Successful Growth

Develop a clear and well-defined strategy for your business. **Figure out:**

What you want to do. Determine how you will create competitive advantage by:

- Having a cost structure that is significantly lower than your competition, or

- Differentiating your product/service offering so that customers are willing to pay a premium for it

How you will get your people to do it.

- Establish clear goals

- Develop a plan to achieve those goals

- Set deadlines for delivery and establish clear accountability

- Cascade the goals throughout the organization

- Ensure human systems work in concert with the plan

Part Three:
Transitioning from a Micro Business to a Small Business

As discussed earlier, when a business transitions from micro to small, the primary change is that the principal ceases to be a "Doer" and becomes a "Manager." Others do most of the primary work of the business, but those others have to be managed. As illustrated in the chart below, doing the primary work of the business is no longer a critical part of the principal's job description. He or she will have to let go if the business is to grow.

As the business migrates from micro to small, the principal will typically retain responsibility for most important tactical decisions and will certainly continue to be accountable for establishing the strategy that drives the business. "Deciding what to do" remains the job of the principal.

However, "Getting it done" no longer means that the principal does it himself or herself. Rather, it now means getting other people to do it. The principal will have to function as a manager. Unfortunately, as many would-be managers have discovered this isn't as simple as barking out orders to just any randomly selected group of people. The principal must first, get the right people in the right job, and then, effectively manage those people.

As you can see in the chart (*see page 90*), there are four things that the manager of a successful small business must do. By the way, the complexity of the principal's job just increased significantly. One element dropped off the responsibility list—doing the primary work of the business. At the same time, two new

Principal's Responsibilities

	Micro	Small	Midsize
Doing the work of the business	✓	🚫	
Make tactical decisions	✓	✓	
Develop strategy	✓	✓	✓
Get the right workers in the right jobs		✓	
Manage workers		✓	

ones appeared—getting the right workers in the right jobs and managing workers. We'll go into more detail on each of the two new elements in the next two chapters.

Transitioning from a "Doer" to a "Manager" requires the principal to operate in an entirely new way. The key to the success of the business ceases to be how well the principal executes the primary work of the business and becomes how well he or she performs the functions of a manager. Unfortunately, the transition is not always an easy one. When principals struggle with this transition, it is either because they are unwilling or unable to step into their new role as a manager or because they are unaware of the need to do so.

Sharon Dabney-Wooldridge, the CEO of KleaneKare, a commercial, industrial and governmental cleaning company, ran headlong into the fact that she had to let go of doing the primary work of her business. She was in the middle of negotiating her first large governmental contract. Her cell phone rang. It was her potential client wanting to talk about the contract. Unfortunately, she was unable to answer the call in time, because she was elbow deep in cleaning a toilet—time to delegate such tasks to others!

Conceptually, giving up doing the primary work of the business is a simple thing. In practice, it isn't always that easy. One reason principals are unwilling to turn over the "Doer" role to others is that they think others don't do it as well as they do. They're probably right. If the principal has grown a micro business to the threshold of becoming a small business, this has happened because he or she is very good at the primary work of the business. If the principal weren't good at the primary work of the business, it would have failed or stagnated before it reached this point.

It isn't unusual to find that the principal is better at the primary work of the business than any of his or her employees. This notwithstanding, if the business is to grow, the principal will have to teach others to do this work, at least, acceptably well. It's important to remember that three employees who are only 90 percent as productive as the principal will still produce 170 percent more than what the principal can do working alone.

While principals who are transitioning the primary work of the business to others may be able to tolerate somewhat lower productivity, they will not want to compromise on quality, nor should they. However, they shouldn't confuse performing a task in a somewhat different way with lower quality. For example, there are multiple ways to close a sale. What works well for one person may not work at all for another. However, if both people are closing sales and gaining loyal customers, the fact that they take a slightly different path to get there is immaterial. Principals need to be willing to transition work to employees who are delivering results, even if they do the work in a slightly different way.

Sometimes principals are unwilling to transition the primary work of the business to others because they simply enjoy doing the work. That's fine, but ultimately they'll be faced with a difficult choice; let go of the primary work of the business or put growth plans on hold. The principal may be able to keep his or her hand in the primary work of the business for a while, but you won't find the CEO of General Motors designing, making, or selling cars. There simply isn't time. Managing the company is more than a full-time job.

We are aware of one situation where the owner of a construction supply company hired a president to run the business. This allowed the owner to focus on the functional area that he enjoyed and at which he excelled—selling. He's great in this role. This arrangement works well for him, but this is admittedly unusual. In most cases, it wouldn't work. In our experience, most owners would not be able to give the president the autonomy he needs to run the business successfully. Much to his credit, this owner is unique and it works for him because he has been able to relinquish control and focus on closing big sales. The principal was able to continue doing the work he loved, but he did have to let go of day-to-day control of the company. One way or another, every growing company will reach the point where the principal has to let go to grow.

Some principals lack the capability to get the right people in the right jobs and/or to manage people once they are in the right job. They may want to hire the right people and be good managers, but they just don't know how to do it. The good news is that you can develop these skills. We'll discuss how in subsequent chapters.

Still other principals are unaware that they need to manage. They want to hire people who don't need supervision. They think, "I don't need to be managed, why should anyone else?" The flaw in this thinking is that, in general, people with enough experience, skill, and initiative to operate completely autonomously are either opening their own businesses or making a lot more money than most small businesses can afford to pay.

We're aware of one principal of a business-to-business company who doesn't believe he should have to manage people. He only hires salespeople with significant industry experience, provides no training, little direction, and expects his people to work autonomously. He's continuously disappointed with his employees, and he will continue to be frustrated until he starts to manage them. There is a reason why companies pay people to manage others. Management is a skill and it isn't something that companies can do without.

For a business to transition from a micro business to a small business and continue to grow, the principal must let go of doing the primary work of the business and become a manager. It's not optional.

6: Getting the Right Workers in the Right Jobs

"First who...then what," has become a very popular mantra in business. The implication of this philosophy is that a company should first employ really good people. Next, it can make decisions regarding the direction of the company and who is going to do what. This may work if you are running a Fortune 500 company where the cost of hiring a handful of very talented people is rounding error on the bottom line. Unfortunately, if you are transitioning a micro business into a small business, blindly following this advice can be fatal.

We spoke with a woman who started a professional service company. She was struggling to grow revenue and to make ends meet. She sought the help of a free counseling service. "If you want to grow your business, first, go hire good people, the work will follow," advised the counselor. Apparently this advisor subscribed to the "First who...then what," mantra. Unfortunately, the young entrepreneur followed the advice...with predictable results.

Lacking revenue, she struggled to make her newly inflated payroll. She first emptied her checkbook and then her savings account. She depleted the proceeds from a second mortgage loan and finally tapped her 401(K). She eventually had to file for bankruptcy protection. While we are sure that much of the advice provided by the free counseling service is very helpful, in this particular case the free service was worth considerably less than was paid for it.

Amazingly, the story has a happy ending. The entrepreneur eventually figured out what to do with the people she had hired. She launched a second business from the ashes of the first. The second business to date is tremendously successful. Yet, if she had figured out where she was going to drive the bus before she loaded it with people (and payroll expenses), she probably would not have suffered the pain and embarrassment of bankruptcy.

We're going to begin this chapter with a premise, which will resonate with many small business owners: You have decided that you need to hire some workers to sustain your business and allow it to grow. You have productive work for them to do. The work will result in the revenue or the cost savings that you will need to pay them and cover your other business obligations while continuing to pay yourself.

Another popular business mantra is to, "Get the right people on the bus." But, telling a business owner to hire the right employees is a bit like telling a college football coach to recruit good players. Thank you very much for that penetrating thrust into the obvious! The question is not whether it's important to get the right people on the bus. We can all agree that it is. The question is: "How do you get the right people on the bus?"

During the research process for this book, we heard a common theme: hiring is a big problem for small and midsize businesses. When we asked one business owner how he ensured that he hired good people, he exclaimed in exasperated frustration, "I don't know. You tell me!" Sometimes the complaint was somewhat more subtle, "It's tough to find good people." Another successful CEO said, "It's a crap shoot when you hire people." We were a little surprised to hear this given that we were researching and writing this book during the worst economy with the highest unemployment rate this country has experienced in our working lifetimes. Yet, there it was.

Principals reported struggling to figure out who would fit well with the culture of their companies and the positions they had available. We heard stories of bad hires—employees terminated for embezzlement, theft and misappropriation of company resources. One business owner shared that he surreptitiously installed GPS devices on all of his trucks. He discovered that many of his trucks were spending large portions of the day in convenience store parking lots. The employees left the motors idling to support the temperature control systems, which burned expensive fuel. Of course, the employees attached to those trucks continued to bill their time to the company. Numerous business owners confessed, "We have made a lot of hiring mistakes." There is general agreement among business owners. To be successful as you transition your business from micro to small, you must get the right people in the right jobs.

We asked small and midsize business owners how they recruited and hired people, and with few exceptions, they were relying on current employees to bring in friends and family to fill the open roles. While we agree that this can be a great source, it is inherently limiting. In one case, the owner of a small HVAC business told us he had hired helpers by simply asking the guys standing by the gate near his business, "Do you want a job? Well then, get in the truck." While this may be expedient in the short-term, it does little to ensure a quality hire. More often, we heard tales of trial and error with little or no methodology for ensuring the firm hired the right people.

> **Determining how to get the right people on the bus is one of the biggest challenges faced by small and midsize businesses.**

Yes, hiring good people can be difficult, but a number of the companies had a clear plan of attack and knew what worked for them. We've incorporated their ideas into these tips on finding the right people for your company. To get the right people, it's important to:

- Know what you need

- Understand what you have to offer

- Cast a broad net with a narrow focus

- Leverage multiple methods and opinions

- Trust, but verify

Know What You Need

Earlier we shared the words of the famous modern philosopher, Yogi Berra, "If you don't know where you are going, you might wind up some place else." A corollary to this piece of irrefutable wisdom is, "If you don't know what you are looking for, you may end up with something else." While it may seem an obvious place to start, identifying what you need is the first step.

Too often, we have seen small and midsize businesses mismanage this step or skip it altogether. They fail to clearly define, with pinpoint accuracy, what they are looking for in a new employee. We've found that most businesses either dive right into hiring with little more than a job title to guide them or spend copious amounts of time developing detailed job descriptions that do little to provide guidance as to what they really need and want.

Telling principals to begin the search for a new employee by specifically defining what the job requires may sound remedial, but it is amazing how many small and midsize business owners skip this critical step or don't execute it well.

Getting clear on what you want begins by defining exactly what you will need the new employee to do. Once you understand this, identify what is required to do the job successfully in each of four categories: (1) physical requirements, (2) experience, (3) behaviors, and (4) cognitive capability.

1. **Physical requirements** – This category includes the obvious kinesthetic activities such as lifting, pushing, standing, walking, bending or squatting. Limit what you specify to the actual requirements of the job. Do not impose unnecessary physical requirements on prospective employees. For example, if a warehouse job requires the employee to be able to put 25-pound boxes on a shelf that is 6 feet high, then say that. Don't specify that the employee must be at least 5 feet tall

because you believe that a shorter person would have trouble putting the boxes on the shelf.

In addition, this category also includes requirements for using the five senses: hearing, seeing, touching, smelling and/or tasting. While this may be somewhat unusual, there are jobs that have these types of requirements. For example, a sommelier should be able to taste and smell differences between various wines. We worked with a printer that required certain production employees be able to see color differences clearly. This company tested prospective employees for color blindness, which was completely appropriate.

Only in very rare instances can or should physical requirements include things such as gender or race. For example, if you were casting the part of Scarlet O'Hara in *Gone with the Wind*, it might be appropriate to require that the actor be a white, female. Except in very unusual situations, considering protected characteristics such as gender, race, religion, age, etc. is not only morally wrong, it's illegal. Employment laws are complicated. We encourage you to seek the help of an attorney or a senior HR professional on this and subsequent steps.

2. **Experience** – This includes work experience, but also any requirement for prior accomplishment such as education, accreditation or licensees needed for a specific job. Most importantly, defining what you want in the category of experience entails identifying what results you want the successful candidate to have demonstrated.

Some jobs have mandated requirements. For example, a job as a general securities salesperson will require a Series 7 license issued by FINRA (Financial Industry Regulatory Authority). To practice law, one must have passed the state bar. Certain nursing jobs require that a person be a Registered Nurse, which requires licensing through the state. Obviously, you must meet regulatory requirements.

With regard to education and work experience, be careful about eliminating good candidates by over specifying. If a job truly takes years of education and/or experience to master, then it can be appropriate to include these as requirements. Examples of such jobs might include skilled artisans, computer programmers or accountants. However, competent individuals can learn many jobs quickly. Don't unnecessarily diminish the pool of qualified candidates by over specifying education and/or work experience.

We worked with a company that was having difficulty hiring people for warehouse positions. They were short-staffed and the jobs were going unfilled. When we examined the job requirements, we found they included the following: high school graduate, minimum of five years of experience working in a warehouse, experience working in a self-directed team environment, etc.

We challenged the job requirements. No. Employees did not need a high school diploma. Instead, the warehouse worker needed to have the ability to count and to match part numbers. Many non-high school graduates can do this. Warehouse experience may have been nice because it indicated that the candidate was aware of the nature of the work. However, the supervisor could teach this particular job to most people in just a few minutes. Prior experience wasn't mandatory.

In the end, the company focused on the physical requirements of the job and behavioral characteristics such as punctuality, a good work ethic and honesty. As the CEO finally stated, he needed people that would, ". . . turn up on time, work hard while they were there and when they leave in the evening, they don't take anything that doesn't belong to them." This change both increased the number of qualified candidates and the quality of the hires. The company filled its open positions.

Get very clear on exactly what you need and want, but don't over specify. Recognize that you can often train people to do the work. An HVAC company with which we worked had been in the habit of hiring only experienced service techs. Unfortunately, they found that they were frequently hiring people who had not succeeded at other HVAC service companies. Often the reasons the new employees were no longer with their previous employers quickly became apparent and the company had to terminate them.

The company changed its hiring approach. It dropped the requirement for work experience and began to hire graduates from the local technical school. The new focus was on hiring based on the desired behavioral qualities. The company had to invest a bit of time in on-the-job training and pair their new hires with more experienced technicians in a sort of apprentice relationship. However, within a few months, they had much better service techs than when they focused primarily on hiring experienced people.

Jacques Moore, the owner of Moore Cadillac, has a similar perspective. He said, "I like to hire technicians from the local community college. They don't have experience, but the good news is that they haven't developed bad habits either. It's tougher to hire experienced technicians."

As you are identifying the experience you need, the qualifications for which you are looking, one of the things you'll want to consider is results orientation. Regardless of the specific jobs candidates have held, do they have a demonstrated record of success? If you want to hire superior people, first define what superior performance looks like in the job you are trying to fill. Then look for people who have a demonstrated record of delivering those types of results. Performance is about results, not about skills and qualifications. Don't compromise on performance, compromise on

> **If you want to hire superior people, define what superior performance looks like and hire people who have delivered those types of results. Performance is about results not skills.**

the qualifications. Define what success means in a particular job and look for candidates who have delivered those types of results.

When screening resumes, there are three primary types: the "Responsible" resume, the "Do" resume and the "Accomplishment" resume. The "Responsible" resume begins almost every bullet point with "Responsible for..." This provides information on the types of jobs that a candidate has attained, but gives no indication regarding whether or not they actually did anything while holding the job. Do you really want an employee whose greatest achievement is that he or she managed to get the job—and it was downhill from there?

The second type of resume we see is the "Do" resume. In this format the candidate begins every bullet point with action verbs such as led, developed, managed, coordinated, etc. This is marginally better than the "Responsible" resume. It does indicate that the prospective employee actually did something. Unfortunately, it says nothing about whether or not what he or she did actually worked. "Developed a marketing campaign," is nice, but suppose sales remained unchanged or worse, declined. That's less impressive.

The "Accomplishment" resume spells out clearly the responsibilities the candidate had, what they did while in other jobs and, most importantly, the results they delivered. For example, "As the Product Manager for widgets, I developed a marketing campaign that led to a 20 percent year-over-year increase in sales."

Perhaps the most important thing that an "Accomplishment" resume indicates is that the candidate focused on delivering results. They believe the results they produced are important enough to include on their resume. Even if you are hiring for an entry-level position, you can look for results. The candidate may not have any relevant work experience. Nevertheless, a statement such as, "While serving as membership chair of the Spanish Club, I increased active participation by 30 percent," indicates that the applicant focuses on delivering tangible results, not just holding a position.

Obviously, candidates must have the credentials regulators require. Experience and education can be important, but don't over specify. When deciding what experience you want in a specific job, make sure you are looking for people with a demonstrated track record of delivering the types of results you need.

3. **Behaviors** – These characteristics include things such as honesty, the ability to work well with others, a willingness to overcome difficulties, attitudes, integrity and work ethic. While employees can learn many skills, it is much more difficult to teach behaviors. Many an employer has failed when trying to convert a lazy person into someone with a great work ethic. If you find that you have to compromise when making a hiring decision, lower the bar on experience or education, but not on behaviors. Hire behaviors. Train skills!

When we asked employers what they were looking for in entry-level employees, the number one attribute was a willingness to learn. Other behaviors ranking high on the list included: listening and oral communication skills, adaptability and creative responses to setbacks and obstacles, self-management, confidence, motivation to work toward goals, a sense of wanting to develop one's career and take pride in accomplishments, group and interpersonal effectiveness, cooperativeness and teamwork, skills at negotiating disagreements, effectiveness in the organization, wanting to make a contribution, and leadership potential. Only one item was education-based and that was basic reading, writing and math ability.

Included in behavior is an assessment of whether the prospective employee would be a good cultural fit with your company. It is critically important to hire people who will work well with other employees. Companies overwhelmingly reported that they would rather have an employee with average skills—but great behavioral characteristics—than an employee with great skills and poor behavioral characteristics. Tom Winfree, the CEO of Village Bank, echoed this sentiment when he said, "We seek to hire people who deserve to work with the ones that are already here." The most talented employee will be detrimental to your organization if they have a bad attitude, are lazy, don't get along with their co-workers or are dishonest. If you want good behaviors, you have to hire them.

> **Hire behaviors, train skills! If you have to compromise when making hiring decisions, lower the bar on experience or education, but not on behaviors.**

4. **Cognitive capability** – As a part of his routine, comedian Ron White frequently observes, "You can't fix stupid!" It's funny, in part, because it's true. An employee can learn new skills, but their underlying cognitive capability is unlikely to improve significantly. So if you want smart employees, hire smart people.

David Gallagher, the CEO at Dominion Payroll, an Inc 500/5000 company, explained that finding the right people became easier when they stopped hiring based primarily on skills and began to focus on hiring smart people who had demonstrated a good work ethic. What we are really talking about is a person's problem-solving capability. How well can someone take the information he or she knows and use it to identify solutions to real-world problems? Smart people are better problem solvers.

Admittedly, people solve problems in different ways. It's important to understand what kind of intelligence you need. Are you looking for an analytic quant-jock or a creative genius? They may well not be the same person. So consider what kind of cognitive capability you need:

o **Analytic** – This person can do the numbers. They are quant-jocks—people who are exceptionally skilled in quantitative analysis. Using algebra to solve business problems is not only easy, it's fun for them—imagine that. In their spare time, analytics sometimes perform regression analysis for amusement. Analysts, scientists and statisticians are usually quite analytic.

o **Structured** – These people are logical. If A and B, then C makes complete sense to a structured thinker. When they reach a conclusion, they can provide a very detailed rationale for their thinking. Most analytic people are good structured thinkers. The reciprocal is not always true. Some very good structured thinkers are not analytic. Many attorneys and computer programmers are very strong structured thinkers.

o **Intuitive** – These people often devise innovative solutions to complex problems. Interestingly, they can't always support their conclusions with a clear rationale. As a result, structured thinkers may tend to dismiss the ideas of intuitive problem solvers. Be careful about dismissing them too quickly. They can sometimes come up with solutions that a structured thinker would never reach. Intuitive thinkers are perfectly able to take two data points and extrapolate to infinity—a proposition that analytics and structured thinkers can't fathom. Such people are often amazed at how frequently the intuitives are right. Further, intuitive problem solvers are often good at understanding how others think. They are frequently good with people. Consequently, they may gravitate to sales, human resources or caregiving professions.

If you want smart employees, hire smart people.

o **Creative** – A creative thinker will often come up with a new angle on an old thought. They are frequently able to connect dots that others don't. In some contexts, creative thinkers can be quite funny because they come up with a completely different take on something that is part of our culture. George Carlin's confusion regarding why we drive on parkways and park on driveways is such an observation. Structured thinking is likely not their forte. Comedians, actors and advertising people tend to be outstanding creative thinkers.

We include this list, while not comprehensive, as a way to push your thinking regarding the type of cognitive capability you need for a particular job. Of course, the types of cognitive capability described above are not mutually exclusive. For example, it is certainly possible for a very intuitive person to be a good structured thinker as well. In fact, all of us have some measure of each of the items listed above. The question is what type of cognitive capability is needed in a particular job and how much of that capability does the candidate have?

Depending on the type of cognitive capability you have decided you need, there are several ways to assess intelligence. Scores on standardized tests, grade point average, major, and educational institution can be helpful in assessing cognitive capability. Further, asking candidates to describe challenging problems they have solved successfully and giving them cases to work through will enable you to assess problem-solving skills.

Some business pundits argue that you don't need to hire incredibly competent people. In fact, they say not only do you not need them; you don't want them. We completely disagree! In our experience, the core of any successful business is good people. These pundits go on to argue that the way to succeed is by building a system that eliminates the need for people to think. We agree that building systems is important as a business grows and we'll discuss this in a later chapter. Nevertheless, our combined fifty-plus years of business experience and our research for this book tells us that good people make successful companies. There is no shortcut.

The first step in getting the right employees for your organization is to identify what you need. Gaining clarity regarding the physical requirements of your job, the necessary experience, which behavioral characteristics are important, and the cognitive capabilities you want your employees to possess will help you to specify what you need. If you have to compromise, relax your requirements on specific job experience and education. Do not lower the bar on results orientation, behavioral characteristics or cognitive capabilities.

Understand What You Have to Offer

Good marketers know that to sell a product or service successfully you have to differentiate it. You have to provide customers with something they value more than the offerings of your competitors. The same is true when you are trying to hire the right talent. You have to market your company to prospective employees. The market for good employees is very competitive, even in a tough economy. It's become cliché to say, "Our people are our most important asset." But, cliché or not, in most businesses, it's true. To attract the right people, you will have to offer something more than the other employers who are courting their services.

One strategy is to offer above-average pay and benefits. Companies that employ this approach justify the generous compensation packages based on the belief that it allows them to hire better people. This strategy can work, but there are two caveats. First, make sure the people you are hiring truly represent top-tier talent. Obviously, paying more and not getting better talent is a bad idea. It is leaving money on the table. No company can afford to do that for long.

Second, ensure that the jobs you are paying a premium for are highly leveraged jobs. That is, be sure that the premium you pay to get the better employee is much less than the additional value they deliver. Even if you get better people when you pay more, it's a losing proposition to put those people in jobs where no matter how well they do; their performance can't justify the premium.

A company with which we worked operated call centers. Through a combination of higher pay, superior benefits and more time off, this company compensated its call-center employees well above industry standards. The company was able to hire and keep good people—arguably people who were much better than average for the industry. Unfortunately, the job of a call-center operator isn't highly leveraged. It just isn't possible to cover the cost of a 40-percent premium by doing a better-than-average job. Over time, this company had to exit the call-center business in large measure. They outsourced the operations, for the most part, to companies that paid market rates.

> **If you are going to pay above-market rates for your employees, make sure that you are getting truly exceptional people and that you are putting them into highly leveraged jobs.**

Conversely, we spoke with Gordon G. Miller, III, who runs G3 Systems, Inc., a technology company. He has found success by paying above-market rates to get unusually talented people whom he puts into highly leveraged jobs. Gordon explained that he can (and has) replaced a team of 11 people, with five people and charged for eight. The customer was thrilled because they saw more than a 25-percent reduction in costs. At the same time, G3 was able to charge a 60-percent premium and thus could easily afford to pay 20 percent above-market rates for its people. When you have a highly leveraged job, paying above-market rates and getting above-average performers can be a win for the customer, the company, and employees.

If you are going to pay above-market rates for your employees, make sure that you getting truly exceptional people and that you are putting them into highly leveraged jobs.

As a small or midsize business, you may find that you can't compete with the big dogs in compensation and benefits, particularly if the jobs you have are not highly leveraged. However, you have other things of value to offer that can help you to attract good employees. Many of the smaller firms we interviewed spoke of offering flexible schedules, giving less experienced employees real responsibility, having a family feel, an entrepreneurial culture, and teaching employees new skills as they grow with the company.

For example, consider a small healthcare organization that was looking for a Registered Nurse (RN) to fill a skilled position required by state regulation. The small business could not afford medical benefits or compete with the compensation offered by local hospitals and nursing homes. However, the business was able to find an RN who wanted a change from the corporate environment she had worked in for more than 15 years. This recently divorced mom valued the flexibility she could arrange with the small business that was against policy in the larger corporate environment. She was willing to take a slightly lower salary to gain some flexibility in her schedule, an attribute that she considered more valuable than a bit more pay. It was a win-win for both employer and employee.

Matching the environment of the company to the type of employees it needs can work wonders. Madison + Main, a midsized marketing, promotion and advertising firm, created a unique environment that has been quite attractive to the very creative people they need to hire and retain. Chief Idea Officer Dave Saunders explained that a combination of free soft drinks and snacks, Friday afternoon beer pong, paid time off for community service, and an annual company cruise to Mexico has allowed his firm to attract and keep the talent it needs to fuel exponential growth. This probably wouldn't work for a public accounting firm, but then Madison + Main is the antithesis of such an organization.

> Although small and midsize businesses may not be able to compete with their larger neighbors in compensation, they have other value to offer.

Make sure you know how you will differentiate your offer from those of firms pursuing the same candidates. If you are going to offer better-than-market compensation and benefits, make sure it's justified by hiring exceptional performers and putting them in highly leveraged positions. Don't discount the value of the experience you provide to your employees. Take a look at your culture and what you, personally, as the principal can offer. Be prepared to sell this to your prospective employees.

Cast a Broad Net with a Narrow Focus

You know what you need and want in a new employee. You can articulate the physical, experiential, behavioral and intellectual characteristics you need. You have also identified what you have to offer. You know why the right employee should come to work for you rather than someone else. Now where do you look to find the right employee? The best way to identify good candidates is to cast a broad net with a narrow focus. That is, review a lot of resumes or applications, but because you know exactly what you are looking for, quickly eliminate the bulk of the prospects and focus your attention on the promising few.

Most small and midsize businesses depend on current employees to refer prospects for open positions. Used properly, this can be a good source of qualified candidates. Used improperly, this can be quite dysfunctional. For example, we worked with a company that instituted a bounty system for referrals that led to hires. If the company hired someone suggested by an existing employee, the referring employee received a fixed amount of money. The employee was not penalized for referring individuals whom the company did not hire. Worse, if the company hired the referred employee, but the employee didn't work out and had to be terminated, the referring employee still received the bounty.

This policy led a number of employees to refer anyone they knew who had a pulse. Those doing the referring did not prescreen whatsoever. The problems and unnecessary work created for management and human resources isn't hard to imagine.

Conversely, Health Diagnostic Laboratory (HDL), a company that provides diagnostic testing services, has found a creative way to increase the effectiveness of its referral program. When a position comes open, management briefs the staff on the job opportunity and asks them to provide referrals.

However, when an employee presents a referral, the first person interviewed is the referring employee. By interviewing the referrer, HDL can determine how well the employee knows the candidate. By asking specific and pointed questions about the candidate, the company can collect a significant amount of pertinent information before ever speaking to the prospective employee. Broad general questions will lead to comments like, "Oh, John would be great." But, if asked, "Could you tell me about how John handles conflict with his coworkers?" The employee is more likely to disclose what she or he knows about John's ability to work well with others.

Further, because the referring employees know that management will interview them regarding referred candidates, they are more selective when submitting a prospect's name. The screening process is automatically honed because employees who refer people that aren't a good fit are counseled regarding the reasons. CEO Tonya Mallory explained that the process has resulted in many high-quality referrals with little to no work expended on prospective candidates who are obviously a bad fit for the organization.

Gordon G. Miller III, the owner of G3 Systems, Inc., who we mentioned earlier, has taken the referral system one-step further and turned it into a process that supports retention. When the company hires a referral, there is a six-month probationary period. If the new hire is progressing well, the referring employee receives an ongoing commission at the end of the probationary period. The commission remains in effect until the referred employee leaves the organization. This creates an incentive for the referring employee to encourage the employee they referred to stay with the firm. Admittedly, such a system would not work well in every environment, but because G3 bills its people's time at multiples of their pay, it can afford the additional compensation associated with hiring and retaining a referral.

In some industries, the most skilled workers know each other. In these cases, referrals alone may be sufficient. For example, we spoke with Mike Manning who runs a masonry company of substantial size. There is no more than one degree of separation between one of his employees and any other bricklayer in the area. Good bricklayers know who can and who cannot lay bricks well. They are able to attract, screen and hire a qualified workforce through the referrals of their employees alone.

If referrals provide your company with a sufficient pool of qualified labor, that's great. However, if you struggle to find the talent you need, you may not be casting your net broadly enough. In small and midsize companies, qualified employee referrals will typically result in a trickle of candidates. For a company that is not sure what they are looking for in a new employee, the trickle can be a blessing because it means they don't have to sort through hundreds of resumes that all look the same. Conversely, if you know specifically what you need, eliminating prospects that are off the mark is an easy thing to do. If you have a narrow focus, you can afford to cast a broad net.

There are many possibilities. Figure out what works best for you and your business. Try advertising in the local newspaper and utilize online sites such as Craig's List and Monster. Develop relationships with the placement offices of local colleges, high schools and technical schools as appropriate. These efforts will bring you more candidates, but if you know exactly what you need, sifting through large numbers of resumes or applications is quick work. Obviously, considering more candidates increases the possibility that you will find the optimal recruit. Stack the odds in your favor. Cast a broad net, but have a narrow focus.

> **Referrals can be a good source of potential employees, but it's wise to consider a broader set of candidates.**

Leverage Multiple Methods and Opinions

At this point, you know what you want in a new employee. You have determined why the right candidate should accept your offer. You have cast your net broadly. You have reviewed literally hundreds of applicants. However, because you have a narrow focus, you have quickly selected the few candidates that, on paper, seem to be a good fit with what you need. The live evaluations come next. How do you conduct these evaluations to maximize the probability that you end up with the right person in the right job?

One of the messages we heard loudly and clearly from Harry Garmon, a well-respected and seasoned business owner, was don't trust your own opinion alone. Too often, owners of small and midsize businesses will select the finalists from a pile of resumes, interview each candidate themselves and make a decision alone. No one else is involved in the process.

Harry says that after years of experience trying to figure out how to get the right person in the right job, he has concluded that the best procedure is to leverage multiple methods of evaluation and get opinions from a range of people. Once he has collected all of this information, Harry takes the feedback and makes the decision himself. But, he pays very close attention to the input he gets from disparate sources. We'll touch briefly on what opinions other than his or her own the principal should consider and then discuss how to leverage multiple methods.

Generally, the hiring manager and at least one other person should be involved in the interview process. The other person can be a subject matter expert, a human resources person, an outside adviser, a person who will be a peer of the new hire or even a subordinate. The vital ingredient is that there is at least one interviewer other than the principal and for critical positions, it may be better to obtain input from additional people.

There are several reasons to have a second opinion during the interview process. First, you will get a better result when a second person can offer insight into the process. He or she may hear or see something that you did not. He or she may ask a follow-up question that would not have occurred to you. However, the most important reason is defensibility. The hiring manager should never be the only person involved in resume screening, interviewing and selection. In our litigious times, it's too easy for an unsuccessful candidate to claim bias when only one individual is involved in the hiring process. Increasing the participation in the selection process reduces this possibility. While the hiring manager should generally make the final decision, it is prudent to involve at least one other person in the process.

We have found that, depending on the job, there are three useful methods of evaluation: (1) interviews, (2) assessments, and (3) simulations and trial employment. We'll cover each below.

1. **Interviews** – We break interviews down into three types: resume interviews, behavioral interviews and cases. A resume or a history interview is the most common type. As the name implies, it involves asking questions about the specifics of a candidate's resume and things she or he has done in the past. Unfortunately, many such interviews result in the candidate regurgitating what they wrote on their resume. Assuming you have actually read their resume, this is of little use.

   > **Getting input from multiple people and using several different methods for evaluating candidates will improve the quality of your hires.**

   What's needed are a specific, preplanned set of questions that help you determine whether the candidate possesses the attributes necessary for success in the job. For example, if you have determined that you need an employee who is results-oriented, you might ask the candidate, "What was your greatest accomplishment and why?" Depending on the response, it may be important to dig deeper. You may need to clarify the candidate's role in the accomplishment. Did he or she really do the work, or did others do most of the work and he or she only participated as a team member?

You can also use these interviews to understand the chronology of jobs if it isn't clear from the resume. Are there gaps where no employment is listed, and if so, why? What was the candidate doing during those periods? It's also frequently helpful to find out why a candidate left each job that she or he has held. Verify these answers during reference checks—don't skip this step.

Use behavioral interviews to get real examples of how prospective employees handled specific situations. The questions in such an interview frequently begin with the phrase, "Tell me about a time when..." As with a resume interview, it's important that you tie the questions to what you are looking for in a candidate. Questions should have a specific purpose.

Consider the case where you are hiring a receptionist. You've determined that the job requires the successful candidate to juggle multiple balls at one time (e.g., while working on a project stuffing envelopes, the phone rings, and a visitor walks up to the reception desk). To test for this skill you might say, "Tell me about a time when you were working on something and there were multiple interruptions. How did you handle that situation?" An answer that contains the phrase "OMG, I freaked out" would not be considered a strong response. What you are looking for is a person who remained calm, prioritized well and successfully handled each issue in turn.

When conducting a behavioral interview, push for detail and make sure there aren't inconsistencies in the story. One candidate described an interpersonal situation with her peer Dave. Later in the conversation it came out that Dave was her boss. Such inconsistencies can be indicative of a fabricated response.

Cases are a type of interview tool used to determine how a prospective candidate solves problems. Typically, the interviewer uses them to assess structured thinking, creativity and/

or analytic ability. When giving a case, the interviewer describes a situation and asks the interviewee to solve the problem. This can be a powerful tool, but again, link the case situation to the job requirements.

For example, if a job requires strong analytic ability, a case that requires the candidate to use basic algebra to solve a business problem may be quite appropriate. However, if the job does not require this type of analytic skill, there would be little point in eliminating candidates because they could not solve such a case. Make certain the case is appropriate given the requirements of the job.

In addition to determining the type of interview to use, you will need to determine the format of the interview. You can conduct interviews over the phone, via video conferencing technology, or in person. You may want to interview candidates one-on-one or use a panel to screen them.

Telephone interviews can be quick and cost-effective, particularly if the candidate would have to travel a great distance to get to the interview. They can be an effective way to screen candidates prior to investing in a battery of face-to-face interviews. The downside is that you don't get to see candidates. Therefore, you can't assess things such as body language and personal grooming. Video conferencing technologies such as Skype can help to address this issue by allowing the interviewer to see remotely located candidates.

One-on-one interviews are the most traditional. Be sure to ask the questions and let the candidate do most of the talking. One tactic clever interviewees will use is to try to get the interviewer to spend most of the time talking. Since many people like to hear themselves talk, most interviewers would see the candidate favorably. Unfortunately, they will not have gotten the information needed to assess the candidate.

In a series of one-on-one interviews, you can have multiple interviewers ask the same question and compare what they hear. Was the interviewee consistent? You can also have one interviewer check for a fit on a particular dimension while other interviewers explore different dimensions. For example, have one interviewer explore the way the candidate relates to her or his peers using a behavioral interview, while a second interviewer assesses analytic ability using a case.

Group or panel interviews can be useful because multiple people will hear the same response. Often, people hear the same thing differently. Multiple perspectives can provide additional insight. A downside to group interviews is that they tend to make some candidates nervous.

Regardless of the type of interview, the most important element is preparation. First, read the resume or application thoroughly before meeting the candidate. This sounds like remedial advice, but it is amazing how many people skip this step and just wing it. Second, plan the interview. How will you find out if the candidate possesses the characteristics you have decided are important for success in the job? What questions will you ask? There are some questions that are illegal or ill-advised. Check with an attorney or qualified HR professional for advice on what you can and cannot ask. What case will you use? Good interviews don't just happen. You must plan them.

2. **Assessments** – There are an extraordinarily large number of assessments available for pre-employment testing. Many are quite useful. There are assessments that measure intelligence, behavioral characteristics and specific skills such as analytic ability. They range in price from free to thousands of dollars. These tools can assist in identifying characteristics and capabilities that may predict success in your organization.

We'd like to tell you to use your discretion when choosing assessments. Unfortunately, it's not that simple. There are an amazing array of rules and regulations that govern the use of assessments for making employment decisions. Just be sure to check with an expert, such as an experienced and competent human resources professional, before deciding which assessments to use.

3. **Simulations and trial employment** – It is very effective to test employees by having them do the actual work of the job. If the job requires data entry, you can ask candidates to input sample data to check for speed and accuracy. If the job requires lifting 20-pound boxes and putting them on a 6-foot-high shelf, you can ask prospective employees to demonstrate their ability to perform that task for a short time.

Cathy and Steve Denunzio own a Goddard School. Obviously, hiring the instructors who will teach the children in their care is critically important. Cathy and Steve require prospective teachers to prepare a lesson plan and teach a class while being observed by an evaluator. This gives them the opportunity to assess the teacher's skills in an actual classroom situation prior to making a decision to offer them employment.

In situations where it's not practical to have the candidate actually do the work, there may be benefit to ensuring that the prospective employee understands clearly what the job entails. This is called a realistic job preview. For example, Stratton Metals is a company that recycles scrap metal. The work is dirty. It's hot in the summer, cold in the winter, and doesn't stop when it rains or snows. Owner Bill Stratton explained that he gives prospective employees a tour of the operation so that they can see the physical requirements of the job and the work conditions. He gives them a very realistic job preview. Some candidates opt out at that point, but Bill points out that it is better than going to the trouble of hiring a person who quits a few weeks later because they don't like the work or the environment.

Another option that works well for many businesses is trial employment. In situations where it won't cost much to have an employee perform poorly for a brief period, it may make sense to simply hire the candidate and see how they work out.

For example, many companies that have commission-only sales jobs follow this procedure. The company invests little to nothing in training. There are no benefits and the company doesn't provide leads. The company pays the employee only when he or she sells something. In such situations, the hurdles to being hired are often quite low. If the new salesperson succeeds, both the company and the employee benefit. If the new salesperson fails, the cost to the company is quite modest. The company has probably paid almost nothing in commissions. Further, poor performers, because they are earning so little, will usually quit on their own.

We would like to issue one caution regarding trial employment. Depending on the laws of your state, you may owe unemployment compensation if the employee works enough hours and you subsequently terminate him or her. This can be a significant expense. Before using trial employment, make sure you understand any costs that factor into the equation. An employment law attorney or competent senior human resources professional can help you with this.

An alternative to hiring a trial employee directly is to utilize temporary services. By using a temporary service to provide the trial employee, the company can avoid the paperwork associated with actually hiring a new employee. Further, it saves the company from having to worry about unemployment expenses.

We worked with a back-office processor of financial transactions that utilized a temporary service to supply all of its needs for new processors. There were several advantages. First, the time it took to find a new processor dropped dramatically. The temp agency kept its pipeline full of interviewed and screened people waiting for work. With just a phone call to the agency, a new employee would show up for work the next day. When the company went through its own human resources department to hire a processor, the time from request to the new hire arriving was usually four to six weeks.

The company did have to pay a premium above its normal hourly rate when it used the temporary employees. However, the company did not pay benefits to these employees. As it turned out, the incremental amount paid to the temp agency was approximately equal to the cost of the benefits it saved. Therefore, there was no net cost to the company for using the temp agency.

When the company brought processors on board, it sent 100 percent of their work through quality control. If the temporary processor did not meet acceptable standards in terms of productivity and quality, the company terminated his or her employment quickly without cost to the company. If the temporary processor did meet productivity and quality standards, the company made sure the prospective employee also met their behavioral requirements (e.g., that the employee was punctual, got along well with coworkers, etc.). If so, the company could hire her or him without additional payments to the temp agency after a negotiated period.

Depending on the situation, pre-employment simulations and trial employment can be effective mechanisms for identifying the right people for your team. For obvious reasons, there are many positions, such as management jobs, where such an approach would likely not be a good idea. Still, for front-line employees, pre-employment simulations or trial employment can often provide a valuable opportunity to assess skills and performance.

To get the right employee into the right job, you must have a robust evaluation process. Leveraging multiple evaluation techniques and getting input from more than one person will significantly reduce the probability that you make hiring mistakes. Having completed the evaluation process, the last step before extending an offer to the prospective employee is to verify employment, check references, perform criminal background checks, look at credit histories and verify degrees that the candidate claims.

Trust, but Verify

The headline in the business section of our local newspaper screamed, "Embezzler is charged again." It jumped off the page at us. Again, what do you mean, again? How does a convicted embezzler get a job where they can do it again? That's like employing a fox to guard the henhouse!

As we read, the horror intensified. Apparently, a small medical practice employed a twice-convicted embezzler as their bookkeeper for four years. Read carefully; not twice charged—twice convicted! Here's a shocker; it looks like she did it again. This time, the woman is charged with bilking her employer out of about $300,000. We can only assume that the medical practice didn't do a criminal background check.

Unfortunately, this small business is not alone. We spoke with numerous employers who discovered employee theft only by chance and long after the company suffered considerable damage. During our interviews, we heard far too many such stories. While almost all businesses can fall victim to employee theft, due to the organization's size and often limited resources, smaller businesses suffer more. One surprising statistic from the Small Business Administration states that employee theft is the cause of 30 percent of all business failures.

In our experience, most small and midsized businesses don't have hiring practices that weed out obvious bad hires—like those who have been convicted of embezzlement or substance abuse, have other criminal convictions or a poor credit history. Smaller organizations are frequently reluctant to spend resources on the types of checks that can identify the bad apples before they find their way into the company barrel. This can be penny-wise and pound-foolish. Saving a few dollars now could cost plenty down the road. Spend the money to perform criminal background checks, drug tests and credit checks.

Sadly, criminal offenses aren't the only dishonesty from which employers need protection. Mysteriously, a successful college football coach cleaned out his office late one night and was gone before morning. He was never seen at the school again. The CFO of an electronics distributor was dismissed without comment. What do these two actual events have in common? Both were the result of an employer discovering that the employee had lied on his resume. Each had represented that he had earned a master's degree when in fact he had not.

When presenting their credentials, prospective employees want to show themselves in the most favorable light. That's natural, expected, and there is nothing wrong with it. It's just good marketing. However, when good marketing crosses the line into intentionally leading others to believe things that aren't true, that's a problem.

Most people understand that outright lies are wrong, but using clever wording to mislead people intentionally is no better. One executive proudly proclaimed that he had graduated from Harvard Business School (HBS). The executive clearly intended to cause people to believe that he had earned a Harvard MBA. At Harvard, the MBA program has very high admissions standards and requires a lot of hard work over a two-year period to complete successfully.

In fact, the man had "graduated" from an executive education seminar conducted at HBS. The program took one week to complete, the primary requirement for admission was having the wherewithal to pay the cost of the program. The only requirement for "graduation" was attendance. Clearly, his accomplishment was a far cry from earning an MBA from the prestigious school. The executive might argue that he hadn't lied because he had actually "graduated" from HBS. Perhaps, technically, he hadn't lied, but the intent to deceive was clear. The company terminated the executive for unspecified reasons. Verify all claims of degrees with the school before you extend an offer of employment.

Protect yourself and your business from deceptive practices by verifying candidates' claims.

Another equally misleading practice is claiming to have a degree from one of the all-too-prevalent diploma mills. Such enterprises have names that sound like legitimate academic institutions. The programs most often require little or no academic work and grant credit for "life experience." These "schools" are not accredited and many will perpetuate the fraud by providing a phone number that prospective employers can call to verify the degree. Make sure that all schools are accredited by one of the five regional accrediting organizations. It's not hard to check— learn how.

Worse, there are now services that will answer the phone as a "former employer" and give whatever reference the prospective employee has paid them to provide. When checking references, don't just use the number provided by the candidate. Make sure you are calling a real company and not one collaborating with the prospective employee to perpetrate a fraud on you.

When checking references, it is a good idea to get to the second and third levels. Most people are clever enough to provide references who will say positive things about them. By all means call these people. However, also speak to selected people not provided by the prospective employee. For example, if the prospective employee does not provide his or her direct supervisor at his or her last several jobs, that's a red flag. You probably want to speak with those people.

When conducting reference checks: use the information that you have collected from the evaluation process to ask very pointed questions. For example, if an assessment suggests that the prospective employee may have a problem respecting authority, ask about their relationship with their former supervisor. When asked broad, general questions most people will give a positive reference. When the questions are pointed and more specific, you are much more likely to get a candid response.

Sadly, statistics reveal that up to 50 percent of resumes contain one or more major misrepresentation. One would hope that moral values and simply doing the right thing would be motivation enough to prevent such subterfuge. Unfortunately, it seems that this is not the case. People who participate in such schemes are likely to come up with a justification for their actions. But deep down, unless they are completely devoid of character, they know that what they are doing is wrong.

The message is clear. In the words of Ronald Reagan, "Trust, but verify." Spend the money to do criminal background checks. Get credit reports if appropriate. Learn how to validate claims of educational and professional accomplishment. The Internet makes this easy and inexpensive. Don't make exceptions! The sad fact is that most employees who steal have a close relationship with their employers.

Do you really want to trust people who would do such things with your customers, your resources, or your money? Don't let fraudsters infiltrate your organization through benign neglect on your part. Make sure that prospective employees are telling the truth, the whole truth, and nothing but the truth.

Ensuring that you get the right people in the right jobs is critical and while it's not easy, it's doable. Bad hires can destroy the business that you have labored to build. The single most frequent concern we heard during our research for this book was that hiring good people is hard. Hiring is a complex task and, unfortunately, you're not always going to get it right. However, following the steps outlined in this chapter will greatly improve the probability that you get the right person in the right job.

Lessons for Successful Growth

Recognize that hiring the right people for your business is critically important. Follow these five steps to improve the probability that your new employees are good ones:

- Carefully define what you need

- Be clear regarding what you have to offer

- Cast a broad net with a narrow focus

- Leverage multiple methods and opinions

- Be aware that deceitful practices are all too frequent—trust, but verify

7: Managing Workers

To successfully transition a business from a micro to small, the principal will move from doing the primary work of the enterprise to managing those who do it. We have discussed how to get the right people into the right jobs. Now let's consider how to manage those people effectively.

As explained earlier, at its core, business involves only two things, figuring out what to do and getting those things done. As a micro business, getting things done meant the principal had to do them. The principal did the primary work of the business. As a small business, getting things done means managing others, so that they do the things you want done. Others now do the primary work of the enterprise. Running a small business involves figuring out what things you want done and getting others to do them. We have long held that, of the two, getting others to do the things you want done is a lot harder.

Managing people is tough. Fortunately, it's a learned skill. Mary had a problem subordinate. Joe had real attendance issues. He was frequently late. He pushed things to the limit, never quite doing enough to make Mary fire him, but always running on the ragged edge. Other than his difficulty arriving on time, Joe was a great employee. Mary was insistent that it

Managing people is tough. Fortunately, it's a learned skill.

was worth the effort to change his behavior. She'd spoken to him about his punctuality in the past, but her complaints were mostly off-hand comments. There might be some improvement for a day or two. Then Joe reverted to his old ways.

Mary went to a class to learn management skills. The instructor taught her not just to complain about the problem, but also to work with the employee to set very clear goals. In this case, the objective was to get the employee to arrive at the office on time or early every day. Mary held Joe accountable for coming up with a plan to achieve the objective. She did not allow him to get away with just promising to show up on time in the future. Rather, Joe had to explain the detailed action steps he would implement that would ensure his on-time arrival.

His plan involved getting to bed at a more reasonable hour and setting his alarm clock for an earlier time. He was going to lay out his clothes before going to bed and make sure there weren't any chores he needed to do in the morning before he left for work. Finally, Joe set a specific time for leaving the house that would allow for possible traffic problems, slow school buses, trains and anything else that might lengthen travel time.

Mary enabled the behavior change by providing appropriate motivation. If Joe started to arrive on time consistently, he would remain employed. Initially, Joe and Mary met first thing each morning to assess performance. These meetings were very brief. Mary simply asked if Joe had any trouble getting in that morning. As time passed and Joe demonstrated that he could consistently arrive on time, the meetings became weekly and then monthly. An amazing thing happened. Joe began to turn up for work on time, not just for a day or two, but for weeks and then months. His behavior change became permanent. Mary had saved her employee from termination. It was a win for the company and a win for the employee. This may seem a small, even trite example. However, it does demonstrate that management is a learned skill. Further, it illustrates the four steps associated with successfully managing people:

- Set appropriate goals
- Develop a plan to achieve the goals
- Empower the employee
- Assess performance and make adjustments

Admittedly, these four items are not rocket science. They're pretty basic, but all of our years of education, reading books on the topic, practical experience as managers, and the research we did for this book suggests that these four simple steps for managing people work. We've seen it time and time again.

Set Appropriate Goals

In Lewis Carroll's classic story *Alice in Wonderland*, Alice meets the Cheshire cat. She asks the cat, who is sitting in a tree at a fork in the road, "Which path should I take to get out of here?" The Cheshire cat responds, "Which way are you going?" Alice says, "I don't know." The cat answers, "Well, then, any path will take you there." Setting goals establishes a direction for employees; it tells them where they are going so they will know which path to take. It helps them to prioritize their activities and focus their efforts.

In the chapter on developing a strategy for the business, we described setting goals at the company level. The manager must cascade the goals throughout the organization. For example, a company may have a goal to reduce overhead expenses by $150,000 in the second half of the year. The company may expect the finance department to reduce its spending by $25,000. What's important is that the sum of the cost reductions for each department should equal the company objective, or perhaps a bit more to provide a contingency for unexpected events.

Each of the goals at the company level should cascade down to the appropriate employees, so that if each individual employee achieves their objectives, the company will meet or exceed its targets. For example, if a company has a goal to increase revenue to

$7.7 million in the current year, each of its four salespeople might have individual goals of $2.1 million in sales. Obviously, if each of the salespeople achieves their goals, the company will exceed its revenue target.

While most employees will have some goals that are cascaded down to them from management, people should also have personal objectives that go beyond the cascaded company goals. Dave Ingram is the President and CEO of Capital TechSearch, an Inc. 500/5,000 firm that provides contract, contract to hire, and direct placement for information technology professionals. Every employee of the firm has their own individual goals. Dave mentors his employees to make sure they have a good plan for achieving their objectives. He observes, "It's my job to create an environment where my people can achieve their goals."

When setting goals with employees, it is critical that they be WHY SMART goals (i.e., Written, Harmonious, Yours, Specific, Measurable, Action oriented, Realistically high, Time and resource bound). We discussed WHY SMART goals in detail previously.

It is also important that the goals be meaningful to employees. There should be sufficient rewards for goal achievement and consequences for failure. This will ensure that achieving their goals will rise to the top of the employees' "To Do" lists. Ask what they see as the rewards and consequences for each of their goals. You may have to push. When asked to list the reward for achieving a specific goal, an employee might respond, "I'll earn a bonus." That's fine, but push deeper, "What would that mean?" The employee might respond, "It will mean that I can buy the car I have been wanting for years." Fulfilling a long-time want is much more powerful than earning a bonus. Help the employee to find the emotional

Make certain that personal goals have an emotional importance to the employee.

motivation for accomplishing their goals. If there is no underlying motivation for goal achievement, it becomes easy to lose focus. The goals won't drive action.

Upon entering the office one morning, a senior executive asked his facilities manager to get him the detailed plan for the layout of the new parking lot. At about 3:00 that afternoon the executive poked his head into the facility manager's office. She was packing her bag. He asked, "Where are you headed?" She responded, "It's Wednesday. I have to pick up my children from school on Wednesdays." "Oh, right," said the senior manager remembering her weekly schedule, "But where is the parking lot layout I asked you to get to me?" The facilities manager replied, "It's on my list. I'll work on it tonight and have it for you first thing in the morning. I've got to run, I'm late." The senior manager, visibly disappointed, turns and walks away in disgust.

He had needed the parking lot layout for a 5:00 meeting that afternoon with the CEO. The senior manager had assumed that his subordinate would move his request to the top of her "To Do" list. After all, he is the boss. Surely, she would do his work first. Unfortunately, she didn't think that was necessary. He didn't give clear direction. If he had simply said, "I need the plan by 4:30 today," he would have gotten the plan within the timeframe he needed or at least an explanation as to why it wasn't possible. Either way he would have avoided an unpleasant surprise late in the day.

Prior to this example, the goals that we have discussed have been longer-term (e.g., annual, semi-annual, quarterly or maybe even monthly goals). When managing people, it is often necessary to establish more short-term objectives. For example, a manager might tell an employee, "Please get me the accounts receivable aging report by 11:00 this morning." You may view these requests as providing instructions or directions more than setting goals. Nevertheless, they are critical to the smooth operation of any business.

When giving directions, it is important to be as clear and concise as possible. Do not assume that the person to whom you are giving instructions knows what you want. In all probability, your subordinates are not mind readers. Explicitly state what you need, and when you would like to have the task completed. You should also inform the employee of any constraints and make them aware of any resources available. Once you have provided clear instructions, check for understanding. It may be a bit awkward to ask people to repeat the instructions. A better way to check is by asking open-ended questions. For example, in many circumstances, it is quite appropriate to ask the employee questions about how she or he plans to accomplish the task. The answer you receive will confirm whether your employee understands what you want him or her to do.

When giving instructions, be clear and make sure there is understanding. One senior human resources director explained that fully half of the disciplinary matters that ended up in her office had some element of misunderstanding between superior and subordinate. Clarity could have prevented many of these issues. Whether a manager is setting long-term goals or giving short-term instructions, clear communication is critical.

It is critically important to set goals, both professionally and personally. Near the end of his life, H. L. Hunt, the self-made oil billionaire, was asked to name the requirements for success. He answered, "There are only two real requirements for success in life. The first requirement is deciding exactly what you want. Most people never get to that point. They never decide exactly what they want in life, and because of this, they simply go around in circles. The second requirement, after a person has decided what he or she wants, is determining the price that will have to be paid to get it and then resolving to pay that price."

Develop a Plan to Achieve the Goals

After deciding what you want (setting goals), H. L. Hunt's second requirement for success was to put together a plan to achieve what you want. To accomplish a goal, the employee will need to commit to a set of actions. A goal without an action plan is just a dream. It's not real and it's not likely to happen.

In establishing action plans, it is helpful to list the obstacles to achieving the goal. There will always be obstacles to achieving a goal. If there are no obstacles, then why haven't you already achieved your goal? Once you have identified the obstacles, list possible solutions for each. Actions will come out of the possible solutions. Once you have identified all of the actions for each goal ask, "If I execute all of these actions successfully, will I achieve my goal?" If the employee can't answer "Yes" with confidence, he or she will need to do more work. The employee will need to identify additional obstacles, possible solutions and actions.

Once you have identified the action steps, it is critically important that you assign a single person responsibility for execution. In most cases, the responsible party will be the employee with whom you are working. In some cases, it may be another employee. The important point is that one person, and only one person is accountable for each action. More than one person can certainly work on the action step. In fact, the person responsible will often need to get others involved in the process. But, our experience has shown that if more than one person is responsible, then no one is accountable. Point accountability is critical. You should never compromise on this.

It is equally important to agree on a date, and possibly a time, by when the employee will complete each action step. This will create the urgency necessary to get the work done in a timely manner. Each action step will have a completion date. Determine the completion date of the overall goal by looking at completion dates for each action step. Particularly for goals that were cascaded down to the employee, it is important to check that the timing of goal completion is acceptable within the context of the overall organization.

Identify one person and one person only who will be accountable for each action item. Point accountability is critical!

Empower the Employee

Human Resources had established goals for on-time arrival. The company was holding its employees accountable for getting to work as scheduled and disciplining them for arriving late. Unfortunately, as the business grew, the data showed that second-shift employees were arriving on time less frequently.

The head of HR decided to investigate further. First shift ended at 3 p.m. Second shift began at the same time. At five minutes to 3, the head of HR was standing at the time clock. Presently, people began arriving. The top of the hour came and employees continued to stream in one, two, three minutes late. She followed the path of latecomers upstream to the parking lot where she observed second-shift employees circling the lot looking for unoccupied spaces. There wasn't enough parking!

As the first-shift employees left, the second-shift workers would take the open spaces and come into the plant, a few minutes after their shift had started. Some enterprising employees left their cars parked illegally, hustled into the plant, clocked in on time, and went back to their cars to wait for a parking space. While this behavior did get them clocked-in on time, it wasn't really what management was trying to accomplish.

> **Make sure that there is nothing standing in the way of employees achieving their goals and that they have all of the tools they need to succeed.**

With the new emphasis on punctuality, second-shift employees were actually getting to the parking lot in plenty of time to clock-in appropriately, but they had to wait for a parking space to become available. Employees could not achieve their goal of on-time arrival because of the lack of a critical resource—adequate parking. The solution—expand the parking lot!

One of management's responsibilities is to enable employees to achieve their goals. Doing this involves: ensuring that you train employees properly, making sure that they are motivated, and removing roadblocks.

1. **Training** – It is unreasonable to expect employees to succeed if you haven't properly trained them and given them sufficient time to practice the skill. In an ideal world, you identify training needs as a part of the goal-setting process. For example, a salesperson identifies one obstacle to achieving a sales goal as his lack of knowledge of how to sell a particular product line. A possible solution would be for the salesperson to receive training on selling that product line.

   As a practical matter, essentially all of the small businesses we interviewed trained their employees in one or more of four ways. First, suppliers frequently offer training on how to use or sell their products. Obviously, these training opportunities will only present themselves from time to time. However, particularly if you have identified a specific need, take advantage of this type of expert training when offered.

   Second, employees may sometimes seek training from third-party providers such as local community colleges. Companies have different arrangements for paying for these classes and workshops. In some cases, the employer expects the employee to pay. Other companies pay all or part of the training if the employee's work links directly to the course content.

   Third, many of the leaders with whom we spoke offered some type of orientation to new employees. Ed Kassab is the President and CEO of At Home Care, a company that provides home healthcare to its clients. At Home Care provides a three-day orientation for its new caregivers. Ed comes to the orientation program and uses it as an opportunity to communicate the company culture to the new hires.

   Finally, the company often provides new employees, and those learning to perform additional tasks, with on-the-job training

(OJT). The principal or an experienced employee shows trainees how to perform a task and then monitors performance. After trainees demonstrate they can perform the new task competently, the training is complete. It makes sense to document the OJT to ensure that important information isn't omitted unintentionally and that the content is the same every time. Further, as will be discussed later, to succeed as a midsize company, process documentation is important. Documenting training is one aspect of this.

2. **Motivating** – One school of thought is that if you get the right people on the bus, they will be intrinsically motivated—requiring no external motivation. While these high performers will insist on receiving market-rate compensation, they don't require extrinsic motivation. They have drive and can't conceive of doing less than their absolute best, regardless of the circumstances.

That may be true for top performers who are well above average. Unfortunately, most of us don't live on Lake Woebegone. In the real world, the average employee is, well, average. The fact is that the average employee does need extrinsic motivation. The notion that you can remove motivation and people will continue to work hard, because they are intrinsically motivated and it's the right thing to do is one that ignores human nature. In general, people will work harder if they believe there are rewards for good work and penalties for poor work. Elite employees notwithstanding, the vast majority of companies do need to be concerned with motivating their people. Essentially all of the leaders of top performing businesses with whom we spoke had some type of system to motivate the behavior they wanted.

There are many ways to motivate employees. Compensation is perhaps the most frequently used motivator. For example, Bob Schrum, the owner of Flagstop Car Wash, pays his managers a monthly bonus based on profit that can range up to 50 percent of their base pay. Commission plans, profit sharing, bonus plans and employee stock ownership plans (ESOPs) are all examples of using compensation to motivate employees.

Money is a serious motivator, but studies show that only the prospect of receiving money in the fairly near future is a strong enough motivator to change behavior. Once the employee receives the money, its power to motivate ends very quickly, some studies say within a week. Further, the same studies indicate that to truly change behavior, the amount of the incentive must be at least 10 percent of base compensation for the period.

Mort Mumma is a Batteries Plus franchisee with multiple locations. He makes very effective use of incentive compensation. His employees can earn a monthly bonus based on the gross profit generated by their stores. Further, they can qualify for an annual bonus based on the company's profit.

For sure, we all need compensation and it has the power to motivate us. However, we also want and need more than compensation alone. Our work indicates that people want to be recognized, contributing members of a winning team. This means that people want to know the enterprise with which they are involved is succeeding. They want to know their hard work is contributing to that success and they want their efforts to be recognized.

> **Employees want to be a recognized, contributing member of a winning team.**

To demonstrate that the team is winning, companies should take every opportunity to celebrate their successes. Disingenuous celebrations won't work and if a company is underperforming, management needs to acknowledge that reality. However, even when a company is in trouble, if it begins to move in a positive direction, it can celebrate the progress. Celebrations communicate to employees that the company is succeeding, the first of the three things required to motivate.

Second, employees need to understand how what they are doing is contributing to that success. How will they know this? Their manager needs to tell them. If you can't come up with a way that an employee is contributing to the success of the company, then you should ask if you need that position or that employee.

Finally, employees want their contributions to be recognized. Monetary recognition is one way. But, simply saying "thank you" when an employee does their job well can be powerful. Instead of speaking to employees only to correct them, catch employees doing something right and praise them. When you praise an employee, make sure you are specific about what you liked and that you link their behavior to a company or professional goal. It doesn't have to be expensive, but a well-timed gift certificate, recognition at a company meeting, extra time off, or even a sincere "job well done" will go a long way towards motivating employees.

Conversely, failing to make employees feel like recognized, contributing members of a winning team, or worse, explicitly telling them that their contributions aren't valued can be a real de-motivator.

For example, we are aware of a professor who taught seminars to area businesses through the local community college. The college recognized her as the best instructor in the program in which she worked for two of the past three years. When the recession hit, one measure the college implemented was to reduce instructor compensation in spite of the fact that it had been flat for the previous eight years. When the college told its star instructor she would need to do more work for less money, she pushed back. The college administrator shot back, "There are hundreds of people out there who can do your job. If you don't want the work, we'll just find someone else."

Shortly thereafter, the professor resigned. In the aftermath, businesses that had previously worked through the college contacted the now independent instructor directly. After her non-compete agreement expired, the instructor found that she could make more and charge the client less by working directly with the businesses. Had the college not made the instructor feel unappreciated, it would have retained this revenue. Failure to keep employees properly motivated can cost your business dearly.

So far, we've talked about positive motivation. Carrots are good, but our experience is that to be most effective, there needs to be some stick as well. Employees need to know that there are consequences associated with poor behavior and failure to perform. We'll talk more about performance management and providing negative feedback later in this chapter. Our experience is that effective motivation requires balance; rewards are important, but consequences are also necessary. If you build an environment that is skewed heavily to either one or the other it will result in poor performance that will adversely affect the business.

3. **Removing Roadblocks** – A local government agency hired us to improve their performance management practices. In the course of this work, the senior manager told us about Sara and Jane. They had historically been good employees, but of late, their performance was deteriorating. In fact, things had reached the point where they weren't actually getting all their work done. The two were only delivering the work of one and a half people. How could we use performance management techniques to reverse this negative trend?

We devised an innovative, high-tech solution that no one in the governmental agency had tried. We got out of our chairs, walked down the hall, and talked to Sara and Jane. What we discovered surprised us. We had expected to find two slackers with attitudes. Instead, we met two extremely dedicated and hardworking employees. As we talked, we learned the nature of their work had shifted. Historically, they had worked manually, completing paperwork and filing or forwarding it. However, during the past several months, more and more of their work was computer based. Unfortunately, the two women were sharing one computer! This wasn't a performance management problem. It was a resource problem. Lack of resources was a roadblock to success. The agency purchased a second computer and productivity soared.

Astyra is a technology-staffing firm that is run by two hard-working college buddies. Ken Ampy and Sam Young met because they were the only two students at Old Dominion University who were regularly in the dining hall for breakfast at 6:30 a.m. Astyra has been hugely successful. It has been the recipient of countless awards. For example, it was included twice in Inc. Magazine's list of the 500/5,000 fastest growing privately held companies in America.

When interviewed for this book, Ken and Sam explained that they make a conscious effort to remove roadblocks for their employees. They always try to provide their people with the tools they need to do their jobs well, even though that can sometimes be expensive. For example, when an employee requested some costly new technology, they bit their lips, and bought the equipment. But, to whom much is given, much is also expected. Ken and Sam hold their people to very high standards. By removing roadblocks, they are intentionally removing any excuses their employees may have for not delivering the desired results.

It's management's responsibility to remove roadblocks that prevent employees from succeeding. However, management should not try to remove the employee's personal roadblocks, even if they result in performance issues on the job. Only the employee can fix these. Family concerns, financial problems, poor habits and other choices related to an employee's lifestyle may cause performance issues. While you can certainly be empathetic, avoid becoming their counselor. Instead, remain in the role of employer and keep discussions focused on the employee's performance and its impact on the organization.

If your organization provides an Employee Assistance Program (EAP), it may be appropriate to direct the employee to these services for expert help with personal issues. At times health-related problems can affect an employee's performance. If this occurs, you should be aware of the possible legal implications (e.g., FMLA and ADAAA). It is advisable to seek expert advice in such cases. You may also want to consult an attorney or qualified human resources professional if performance issues lead you to consider termination, suspension, demotion or other forms of discipline.

However, many roadblocks are within the employer's control. Such roadblocks include policies, procedures, management practices and the lack of critical resources. For example, one organization with which we worked had a department that required its employees to complete their orders by the end of each business day. A second department had this same requirement. Unfortunately, the second department had a roadblock. It needed the completed information from the first department to do its work and meet the deadline. By simply changing the cut-off time for the first department to noon, we were able to end a long-standing feud, change rivals into teammates, and significantly increase productivity.

Sometimes external factors such as vendor or customer issues can act as roadblocks. We worked with a company that had one such customer. This particular person was unreasonably demanding. He complained incessantly, often with little or no justification. The employee serving this customer was frustrated because she couldn't succeed in satisfying her client. The company was expending significant resources in a vain attempt to please the unhappy man. Analysis revealed that the business was actually losing money serving this customer. Finally, the principal agreed that the best course of action was to "fire" the customer. When customers become the roadblock to success, there are rare instances when it is best to choose not to serve them. Removing roadblocks can allow your employees to be successful.

To maximize the probability that your employees achieve their goals, and therefore your company achieves its goals, you must empower your workers. Empowering employees means three things. First, you must properly train your workers to do the tasks necessary to achieve their goals. Second, you will need to motivate your people. There should be rewards for success and consequences for failure. Finally, you should remove roadblocks that are within the company's control. Following these steps will result in your employees more consistently achieving their goals.

Assess Performance and Make Adjustments

You have worked with your employees to set goals and develop an action plan. You have also taken the necessary steps to enable them to do their jobs well. Now you have to assess their performance and make any necessary changes. We're not talking about annual performance evaluations. A formal write-up may only happen once a year, but effective management requires assessing performance much more frequently. For employees who are new to the organization or learning a new task, you may need to assess their performance daily or perhaps even more frequently. Employees who have demonstrated competence may only require weekly, bi-weekly or even monthly meetings to discuss performance.

The first step in accurately assessing employee performance is to collect information. Become familiar with what is happening in their area of responsibility. Management by Walking Around (MBWA) became popular in the 1980s. The term describes the process of informally checking on your employees by visiting them in their workspace and gathering qualitative information about their work-related issues. This provides context for the quantitative information that you will also collect.

If you have written WHY SMART goals, you'll be collecting measurable performance information that will put you in a position to assess progress toward the goal. When reviewing progress with your employee, there are a series of questions that you'll want to discuss:

1. **Are the goals still appropriate?** Sometimes the direction of the company changes and you will need to set new goals. Massive changes in the environment can cause old goals to become inappropriate. We are always loath to lower goals. We worry that doing so will cause employees whose results are falling short of targets to spend time developing rationale for lowering the bar. We'd rather that they spend their time trying to figure out how to get over the bar in spite of challenges. Our reticence notwithstanding, there are times when goals become unachievable or undesirable and need to be adjusted.

> A formal performance evaluation may only happen once a year, but effective management requires assessing performance much more frequently.

2. **If executed, will the planned actions lead to the achievement of the desired goal?** If it doesn't look like the planned actions will lead to the desired goal, adjust the plan. If you cannot devise a plan that will lead to accomplishing the desired goal, you may need to adjust the goal. There is no benefit to having an unachievable goal.

3. **Are the goals, action steps, responsibilities and deadlines clearly understood?** Remember, one of the most frequent causes of an employee's performance not meeting a manager's expectation is misunderstanding regarding the task, who was to do it and/or when it was to be completed. To ensure that your expectations are in alignment with the employee's, check for understanding by asking open-ended questions. "Do you understand?" is not an open-ended question. The employee can simply answer, "Yes." A better approach would be to ask, "How do you plan to complete the task?"

4. **Is additional training needed?** If you have not trained all of the people involved in executing the action plan, you must

address this issue. It is unreasonable to expect success if those executing the plan aren't properly trained.

5. **Is the person properly motivated?** Make sure the people executing the plan are properly motivated. Are both the carrot and the stick in place? In other words, are there sufficient rewards for success and consequences for failure? If not, you need to establish these.

6. **Have the roadblocks been removed?** If you need to adjust policies or procedures to enable success, change them. If employees lack the tools to do the job properly, acquire the correct equipment. Don't be sucked into dealing with an employees' personal issues, but remove all roadblocks that are the company's responsibility.

If the answer to each of the six questions above is a clear and unequivocal "Yes," but the employee is not making acceptable progress toward the goal, you are left with the inescapable conclusion that the employee is either not capable or not willing.

Sometimes the problem is that the employee is just incapable of doing the work. Some jobs are not suited to certain individuals. Perhaps the physical requirements of the job exceed the employee's capability. The employee may not possess the intellectual capacity to succeed in the role. Maybe the cultural environment or job duties turn out to be a poor fit for the person's demeanor.

If this is the case, employers frequently fall victim to the temptation to move the employee to a new role. This can work out well, but pursue this option with great caution. Before making such a change, make sure that the employee is ready to take on the new challenge. Don't move the employee simply to avoid a difficult discussion. Termination is usually the best course for all concerned. Under any circumstances, you need to examine your selection process. How did an incapable employee get the job in the first place?

Sometimes the person is fully capable, and for whatever reason internal to them, is unwilling to perform. If you have agreed on the goals and the action plan, removed all roadblocks that are internal to the organization, and made sure that the employee is fully trained, motivated and capable, there is only one other reason for underperformance—the employee is not willing to do the work. In such circumstances, the only option is termination. This is often a difficult decision for an employer. In addition, the decision can have legal consequences. If you need to terminate an employee, you may want to seek counsel from an attorney or a qualified HR professional.

Managing people is difficult. It's not an exact science and there is no magic wand that will ensure you always get it right. In fact, you won't always get it right. Even outstanding managers make mistakes. The good news is that managing people well is a learned skill. With work, you can improve your capability in this area. Doing so will take a concerted effort on your part, but if your company is going to thrive as a small business, your skills as a manager will be of paramount importance.

Lessons for Successful Growth

Follow four key steps to manage your people effectively:

1. Set appropriate goals

2. Develop a plan to achieve the goals

3. Empower employees

4. Assess performance and make adjustments

Part Four:
Transitioning from a Small Business to a Midsize Business

When a company is truly operating as a small business, people other than the principal will perform most if not all of the primary work of the business. Transitioning to a small business allows a company to grow well beyond its potential as a micro business. However, the growth that is possible with a small business structure is limited as well.

A business in the IT service field had approximately 70 employees who were doing the primary work of the business. All of these people reported directly to the principal! This is the quintessential small business structure. Not surprisingly, the business was imploding. The formerly profitable business was awash in red ink. The principal continuously canceled or rescheduled meetings due to the heavy demands on his time.

Suppliers described the principal as being distracted and not able to give them the time they needed. He didn't have time to train or motivate his people. Annual performance evaluations were a true nightmare because he had to handle every one of them. He was working untold hours and the business had impinged on his personal life in a major way.

Most importantly, the principal did not always return phone calls from prospective clients. This led to comments from former supporters of the business such as, "I can no longer recommend people to this company. I'm not confident that my referrals will be treated well."

This is what a company looks like when its growth has exceeded the limits of the small business structure. It needs to transition to a midsize business model. A stark choice faced the owner. Unless the business migrated to a midsize management structure, it would stagnate at best and face catastrophe at worst. In the best case, for every new client the business acquired, it would lose one who was unhappy with the now reduced quality of service. In the worst case, inappropriately supervised and inadequately trained employees would make mistakes that might result in expensive remediation or even lawsuits that could ultimately force the business into bankruptcy.

Conversely, consider the local franchise of a business called Comfort Keepers, which is in the home healthcare business. It's owned by Ed and Carol Anne Golden and is similar in size to the business described above. But, Ed and Carol Anne are in the process of migrating their business to a midsize structure. Because of this, Ed has been able to delegate many of the responsibilities that he formerly performed to other managers. He has hired a general manager who manages a scheduler, and a customer service manager. The GM is also responsible for human resources and administrative functions. Further, the principal has an employee responsible for training and quality control as well as a business development person on his staff.

The principal has established a series of processes so that his people know how to do their work. The processes ensure that employees perform tasks in a consistent manner. For example, he has established a process for all client interactions, the completion of paperwork, and the resolution of problems that arise during the course of business. He even developed a booklet outlining the firm's processes, which he distributed to employees throughout the business. These processes have resulted in the principal not having to be involved in much of the day-to-day operation of the business. Employees know what they are supposed to do and they have a mechanism for correcting problems.

Further, the principal has developed a set of metrics so that he can monitor what is happening with the business without having to be personally involved with every detail. He reviews a limited set of reports that keep him up to date on what is going on in the business. If there is a significant issue, it will show up in these reports. When the principal identifies a potential problem at the top level, he can quickly drill down into lower levels of detail. This allows him to understand the nature of the challenge and take countervailing measures.

As a result, the principal is able to sleep well at night, because he knows his business is operating smoothly. While he certainly works hard, the principal has been able to strike a balance that allows a good personal life. Further, it allows him to focus his work time on high value tasks at which he excels, such as finance, marketing, motivating his people, and developing creative solutions for the strategic challenges and opportunities his company encounters. For example, he has developed a pay-for-performance program that means every employee of the company has the opportunity to receive incentive compensation. Further, he has developed a 401(k) plan and a paid time off program to increase employee retention rates in an industry where this is certainly not the norm.

While the IT service company described earlier was imploding, this company is poised for growth. It expects to double its size in the next four to five years. The primary difference is that the successful business is migrating from a small company management structure to a midsize company management structure and the principal has been able to let go of at least some of his day-to-day management responsibilities.

When a company transitions from small to midsize, the primary structural change is that a layer of management is inserted between the principal and those doing the work of the business. The principal is now managing managers. That's the obvious change, but the subtle changes are more important. To succeed as a midsize company, the principal will have to let go of a substantial amount of responsibility. The principal will need to delegate responsibility to the managers that he or she will have put in place. This is a real challenge for many principals.

As can be seen in the chart below, the principal continues to be responsible for setting and driving the strategy of the business. However, he or she will need to delegate much of the tactical decision-making. Many principals struggle mightily with delegating tactical decisions to others because doing so means they also give up a measure of control. They hesitate to trust others with their baby and yet, if they want to make further progress, they will need to overcome this reticence. The principal will have to *Let Go to Grow*.

Principal's Responsibilities

	Micro	Small	Midsize
Doing the work of the business	✓	🚫	
Make tactical decisions	✓	✓	🚫
Develop strategy	✓	✓	✓
Get the right workers in the right jobs		✓	🚫
Manage workers		✓	🚫
Delegate Authority and Hold Accountable			✓
Get the Right Managers in Place			✓
Establish Systems and Document Processes			✓
Develop Robust Metrics			✓

Further, as the company migrates to a midsize structure, the principal has to transition to others many of the management tasks that he or she assumed when the business transitioned from micro to small. For example, the principal should empower the new level of managers to hire their own people and to manage those people once they are in place. If the principal does not transfer this authority to the managers, they will lose substantial control over the results that they can achieve in their areas of responsibility.

If you don't give your people control over the results, you cannot hold them accountable for the outcomes. Ed Kassab is the President and CEO of At Home Care, another midsize home healthcare provider. Ed understands the importance of empowering his managers. He has delegated the hiring, firing, and managing of his company's caregivers to his branch managers.

The principal will have to let go to grow, but the transition from small to midsize isn't all about relinquishing responsibility. There are some new management challenges that arise as he or she transfers tactical decision-making authority, and the hiring and the management of more junior employees to a new layer of managers.

The principal will need to hold his or her managers accountable for the performance of their employees. But, he or she cannot delegate effectively unless the right managers are in place. Delegating to the wrong people can be worse than not delegating at all. Further, the principal needs to develop and communicate documented processes to his or her employees. This is how employees will know what they are supposed to do. Finally, metrics need to be implemented that will allow the principal to know what is going on with the business even though she or he is not intimately involved with every decision.

One of the subtle changes that occurs as a business transitions from micro to small to midsize is that the role of the principal becomes exponentially more complex. Although it is admittedly an oversimplification, it is nonetheless instructive to note the growth in the number of areas of responsibility. As a micro business, the principal had three primary responsibilities. When the business transitioned to a small management structure, the principal had to let go of one responsibility, doing the primary work of the business, but she or he picked up two additional tasks. The number of responsibilities grew from three to four. By the time the business achieves midsize status, the principal's responsibilities will have grown to five.

Further, as a micro business, how well the principal executed the primary work of the business determined the success of the organization. When the company transitioned to a small business structure, the key factor for success became the principal's ability to hire the right workers and manage them well. Managing others is significantly more complex than simply doing the work yourself.

As a midsize company, the principal must manage an enterprise. This entails all of the complexity of managing in a small business structure (i.e., the principal has to hire and manage the people who are managers). In addition, the principal will have to orchestrate the smooth running of the enterprise through establishing appropriate systems, processes and metrics. This is a decidedly different and more complex challenge than the one that faced the principal in either the micro or small business management structure.

In the balance of this section, we will cover the four new areas of responsibility that the principal inherits as the business transitions from small to midsize:

1. **Delegate Authority and Hold People Accountable** – A subtle, but often difficult change is that the principal must begin to delegate responsibility for the day-to-day operation of the company to the managers who are running the functional areas of the business (e.g., the CFO, VP Sales, VP Operations, etc.). As the business migrates from a micro to a small business, the principal has to move from a "doer" to a "manager," but she or he continues to be able to make essentially every important decision in the day-to-day operation of the enterprise. As a company moves from small to midsize, the principal must delegate many of these decisions to the functional managers.

   However, if the principal delegates authority, accountability must go with it. One without the other simply won't work. If the principal holds his or her managers accountable for results, but does not give them the authority to make the decisions that drive results they are likely to become frustrated when results do not meet expectations. They will not feel fairly treated when they are held accountable for things that they can't control because they lack the authority. On the other hand, if the principal delegates authority, but does not hold the managers accountable, results will likely not meet the principal's expectations.

The only thing worse than not delegating when you need to is doing so before you have the proper groundwork in place. We outline this groundwork below.

2. **Get the Right Managers in Place** – As the business migrates to midsize, a new challenge will arise. You must put managers in place. Whether you promote managers from within or hire them externally, this can create hurdles. For example, a loyal employee (or even worse, a partner) who was completely able to function doing the primary work of the organization in a small business structure may lack the skill set to become a manager in the midsize structure. Now, imagine that the loyal employee also happens to be a family member. The principal must make the unhappy choice between bringing a manager in over the loyal employee or managing the person out of the business.

3. **Establish Systems and Document Processes** – As the principal begins to pull back from the day-to-day operation of the business, he or she must establish and document processes to ensure employees perform work in a consistent manner. If the principal does not establish consistent processes across the organization, the result will inevitably be inconsistent performance, and ultimately dissatisfied customers.

4. **Develop Robust Metrics** – Principals can delegate authority and accountability. They can establish appropriate processes. Yet, one thing more is required. They must develop a set of robust metrics to allow them to stay in touch with what is happening in the business even though they are less involved in its day-to-day operation. In spite of delegating to the right people and having documented processes in place to ensure consistent performance, the business will inevitably run into issues from time to time. The principal will need a robust set of metrics so that he or she is aware of the problems in time to take corrective action.

8: Delegating Authority and Holding People Accountable

In a small business, the principal has delegated the primary work of the business to others. However, the principal most often personally manages all of the people to whom he or she has delegated work. Further, the principal frequently continues to make every significant decision, both strategic and tactical.

For example, we talked with the owner of an auto repair business, who employs six mechanics and three people who handle the administrative tasks. All employees report directly to the principal. He is a highly qualified auto technician with years of experience, who has built a reputation for outstanding work and honest dealings. His customers trust him personally and expect his individual attention. He shared with us that he knew every detail of every repair done by his shop. He explained that when customers ask a question about their car, he has to be able to answer without checking records or going to ask one of his employees. Nothing of consequence happens in this shop without the principal being personally aware and involved.

Every employee reports directly to the principal. This is a quintessential small business structure. At this size, the principal is able to manage the operation very well. We were impressed with his business. We would take our cars to his shop with confidence. However, if he grew this business significantly without changing its management structure, (e.g., to two or three times its current size), he would become overwhelmed because it would be impossible for him to stay on top of the details of every job. If he tried, he would have to work an untold number of hours and yet at some point, he wouldn't be able to keep up. He would lose any semblance of a personal life. In spite of super human effort, he would fall behind. Customers would ask about their cars and he wouldn't know the answers. The operation would come unglued. Soon, customers would start to leave and growth would stop.

Wisely, this particular business owner has made a conscious decision not to grow his business beyond its current size. This is a legitimate and reasonable decision. Ultimately, any business owner who decides to grow his or her business beyond the size that can be supported by a small business structure will be forced to go down one of three paths:

1. **Stop growing the business** at a size that a small business structure will effectively support. This was the route taken by the owner of the automobile repair shop described above and the concrete contractor described earlier. It's a viable and a completely reasonable choice. Many people live happy and productive lives managing small businesses and see no need to grow their enterprises beyond this point. We've heard business pundits exclaim that businesses must grow or die. We spoke with numerous savvy entrepreneurs who have debunked that myth by thriving at one size for decades.

2. **Continue to grow the business without delegating** the hiring or management of employees or day-to-day decision-making responsibility. The result will be unhappy at best. As the business grows, the principal will become overwhelmed. There won't be enough hours in the day nor days in the week. Any sort of work-life balance will be a distant memory. The provider of IT services we described earlier where the principal had more than 70 direct reports is a clear example of a company which had grown beyond the size that could be supported by a small company structure. If the business continues to grow, no matter how hard the principal works, things will start to fall through the cracks. The quality of work will begin to suffer. Dissatisfied customers will start to leave. Eventually an unsatisfying equilibrium will be all that is left. New customers will equal unhappy departing customers and growth will stop.

3. **Delegate** the hiring and management of workers, the day-to-day running of the business, and the associated tactical decisions to competent managers who you hold accountable for results. During the course of our research for this book, we had the privilege to speak to the CEOs of a number of very well run midsize companies where appropriate delegation was evident. None exemplified this better than Frank Boehling, the owner of eTEC Mechanical. This company is a mechanical contractor in the commercial, governmental and industrial markets. Frank has delegated the responsibility for various pieces of the business to managers he holds accountable for results. This has allowed the company to continue to grow successfully. It has weathered an economic downturn and remained profitable while doing so. Perhaps most importantly, the CEO has been able to maintain a lifestyle that works for him and his family. Frank Boehling is proof positive that proper delegation can allow a principal to have a successful and growing business while maintaining a satisfying personal life.

> As a business grows to midsize, the principal can maintain a satisfying personal life and continue to grow his or her business *only* through:
> 1. **Properly delegating authority to his or her managers**
> 2. **Holding those individuals accountable for results.**

The principal of a small business that is growing rapidly faces a decision. Three choices are possible. One is to stop growing, but if the business owner wants to continue to grow the business beyond the size that can be supported by a small business structure, only two paths are available. Obviously, one path is preferable to the other. Most business owners will acknowledge that to grow beyond a certain point they will have to delegate. Yet, many principals who want to grow their businesses find it difficult to relinquish this authority.

In the balance of this chapter, we explore:

- Why Principals Struggle with Delegating

- Effective Delegation

- Holding People Accountable

Why Principals Struggle with Delegation

There are several reasons why principals struggle with delegating management and decision-making authority. Sometimes, the reasons can be emotional and not necessarily grounded in reality. Other times, the concerns are very real indeed.

- **Loss of control** – The principals of prosperous and growing small businesses are people who have already successfully delegated the "doing" of many tasks when the business transitioned from micro to small. Yet, they often hesitate when it comes to delegating decision-making authority. One reason is that this equals relinquishing some measure of control of the business.

  Even when principals have delegated doing the primary work of the business to others, if they maintain all decision-making authority, they can also maintain control. It's the loss of control that frightens many principals. Crossing this threshold can be very emotional. They are giving up control of their baby. Much as when a child goes off to college and will, for the first time, be outside of the vigilant supervision of his or her loving parents on a more or less permanent basis. Parents are proud to see their progeny move on to the next stage of life. Their pride notwithstanding, it's still not easy for them to relinquish control of their baby. Parents often find this transition to be gut wrenching.

- **"It's what made me successful"** - It's just common sense. If something works, keep doing it! It would be counterintuitive

> **One of the primary reasons that principals are reticent to delegatedecision-making authority is that they equate it with losing at least some measure of control of their business.**

to do otherwise. But, to be successful as his or her business transitions to midsize, the principal will have to give up doing the very thing that made the company successful as a small business. If the business continues to grow, what caused you to be successful in the past will be your undoing in the future. Many people find it difficult to give up doing the things that brought them success but they will have to *Let Go to Grow*.

- **"No one can do it as well as I can"** – A third reason that principals are reluctant to delegate decision-making and management authority is that they believe no one in the company can do the job as well as they can. They are probably right! The business has been successful and grown to the brink of midsize primarily because of the principal's skills as a manager and her or his ability to make decisions.

  In a well-run midsize business, the principal may well be able to do the jobs of each of her or his direct reports better than each of them can. Nevertheless, if the principal has put the right managers in place, he or she can most assuredly not do all their jobs better than they can collectively. Principals, quite rightly, will not want to compromise quality. However, failure to delegate can actually result in a lower quality outcome because the principal is overwhelmed and simply can't do it all. Even with the best will and intentions, it's not humanly possible. This is one example of where perfectionism can actually be the enemy of both efficiency and effectiveness.

- **Too busy to delegate** – We've witnessed principals who are too busy to delegate. This may sound a bit oxymoronic. Surely, delegating responsibility to others would take less time than doing the job one's self—at least in the long run. Yet, initially, that may not be true. Delegating correctly takes time. The principal must put the right people in place. He or she must train and supervise them and establish clear lines of responsibility. This all takes time.

Principals can well find themselves in a place where it is simply faster to do it themselves. Delegation would actually take more time in the short term. Of course, what is expedient in the short term can create problems in the long term. Sometimes you have to spend a buck now to save five bucks in the future. Failure to delegate because it takes more time is yet another example of the urgent overtaking the important. By the way, it also points out why smart principals delegate before their overly burdensome workload forces them to do so. Once they find themselves in this position, they may well not have time to delegate properly.

Principals are reticent to delegate for a number of reasons. Whatever the reason, they will have to overcome this reluctance, if they wish to maintain a good work-life balance. In addition, the principal will need to delegate to grow the company beyond the size that can be supported by a small business structure.

Effective Delegation

As discussed above, principals are often hesitant to delegate tactical decision-making authority as well as hiring and managing the workers. In many cases, they should be! Before delegating, you must lay the proper groundwork. If it is not in place, don't delegate. Several leaders of businesses that are now successful confessed that they delegated too soon. Invariably, their comment was, "We almost lost the business." Laying the proper groundwork means several things:

- The right managers must be in place so that you can delegate the work to them. These people will need to be well trained, motivated and empowered. A successful manager we know once made the mistake of delegating an important piece of work to a person who lacked the capability to do it. The task required superior analytic skills that the employee did not possess. The result was not a happy one. The employee performed the analysis inappropriately. This led to incorrect conclusions and bad decisions. What followed was a great deal of rework to correct the problem and put things back on the right track. Delegating to the wrong people can be a disaster. Principals should not delegate until the right people are in place.

• Processes will need to be established to communicate to the organization how things are to be done. Without the clarity created by well-documented processes people will, quite naturally, do things in the way that seems best to them. The inevitable result will be inconsistent performance and an operation that spirals out of control. Dr. Dodd Levy, the CEO of CarePoint Medical says, "Don't assume that others are functioning the way you would." He's right. You need process to ensure that employees understand how you want things done.

• Robust metrics need to be developed so the principal knows what is going on in the business without being personally involved. Without robust metrics, it can be months before performance issues come to the principal's attention.

Consider an automotive parts distributor. Pressure to improve cash flow by reducing inventory was great. Unfortunately, lower inventory resulted in stock outs; shipments were delayed. Customers who depended on timely deliveries became frustrated and eventually started to take their business elsewhere. Without appropriate metrics, the principal was not aware of these issues until he saw the decline in sales reflected in the monthly P&Ls. By this time, it was too late. Had the principal received weekly reports containing metrics that revealed increasing stock outs and reduced on-time shipments, other action might have been taken in time to save the customers. Bernard Robinson the principal of a midsize business that provides IT networking support services highlights the need for effective metrics to monitor performance by saying, "Delegation without follow up isn't management."

Once the appropriate managers are in place, developing appropriate processes and establishing robust metrics are critical. We will discuss each of these in greater detail later in the book. It is critical to get this fundamental groundwork in place before delegating authority and responsibility. Once you have established this groundwork, there are several tips that are useful when delegating responsibility to others.

One Friday afternoon, Sarah said to Tom, "I believe that you could run the daily production meeting." Sarah believed she had delegated the running of the production meeting to Tom. He understood that his boss had expressed faith in his abilities, but not that she had delegated the job to him. On Monday morning the production meeting didn't happen because Sarah wasn't there to run it and Tom didn't understand that she expected him to do it. Be explicit about delegation. Explain to the employee in very clear terms that they will be responsible for the delegated item going forward.

To delegate effectively:
1. **Get the right managers in place**
2. **Document processes**
3. **Establish robust metrics**

When delegating responsibility to others, it is best to begin by explaining very clearly what results you expect. Once you have explained the task, check for understanding by asking open-ended questions. For example, the purpose of the production meeting discussed above was to make changes to the production schedule to allow the plant to fill critical orders while minimizing disruptions. There was an expected outcome or result.

Sarah might have said to Tom, "I would like you to run the production meeting on Monday morning. It is important that this meeting result in all necessary changes to the production schedule. What are your thoughts on how you would conduct the meeting to make sure that happens?" Whenever possible, results should be quantified and objective. This may not always be possible, but it is always a useful objective toward which to strive.

Once the desired results are clear, set the employee up to succeed by providing any necessary training, coaching or instruction. Don't do what we call "the dump and run." Don't pass responsibility to someone else and then ignore him or her. Rather, it may be a good idea to supervise the employee closely the first few times he or she handles the newly delegated task. At the same time, be careful of micromanaging. Once the employee demonstrates that he or she can successfully execute the delegated task, let go of it.

Another way to set up your employees to succeed is to remove roadblocks to their success. At a minimum, this means ensuring they have the right tools to do the job. Don't send a man with a shovel when he needs a backhoe. The shovel operator may be able to get the job done, but the principal is unlikely to be happy with the time it takes to complete the work.

In addition, removing roadblocks also means resolving organizational conflicts that prevent success. For example, in one company the payroll department was responsible for having paychecks ready by 4 o'clock on Friday afternoons. However, getting timesheets completed in a timely manner was not a high priority for operations—they had their own work to do. Payroll often received the timesheets too late for the paychecks to be ready by 4. Therefore, the payroll department was often unable to achieve its goal. Clearly, it would continue to be unable to achieve its goal until management resolved the conflict. Ultimately, management established timesheet delivery deadlines. Payroll would not process timesheets received after the deadline until the next week. Amazingly, getting timesheets in before the deadline became a priority and the payroll department was able to achieve its goal.

We worked with one company where the principal "delegated" tasks to his direct reports. Unfortunately, he also continued to micromanage, insisting that employees change the smallest details of their decisions to suit his preference. For example, the principal assigned one of his direct reports the responsibility for organizing the annual sales conference. Salespeople from all over the country were meeting off-site in a hotel near the corporate headquarters. To save money, the company asked those employees coming from out of town to share rooms. The principal saw the room assignments after the direct report had communicated them to the sales force. He immediately insisted on a number of changes. No doubt, there were good reasons for the changes. But in reality, who roomed with whom was not of huge importance. The principal could have left the subordinate's decisions intact with little detrimental impact to the conference.

Unfortunately, this type of micromanagement was not an isolated instance. The principal repeated this behavior with great frequency. It left the management team neutered. No one was willing to make a decision without the principal's approval because doing so might well result in embarrassment when he publicly reversed the decision.

There is a cost associated with usurping authority that you have delegated to an employee. You teach employees not to take any initiative and much, if not all, of the benefit of delegating is lost. This leaves the principal to make every decision or worse—decisions won't be made at all. If a principal is going to successfully delegate, he or she must allow the employee the latitude to make decisions even if they are different from what the principal would have done.

We're not suggesting that a manager allow subordinates to do things that will, with a high degree of certainty, have a materially adverse effect on the company. But, before reversing a decision that has been delegated, make sure the benefit significantly outweighs the cost. By the way, if this happens often, there is a problem. Either the task has been delegated to the wrong employee, the objectives are not clear, or the employee has not been properly instructed regarding how to execute the task.

Finally, make sure that your managers share your vision for the direction of the company. Thoroughly imbue them with the culture you want your company to have. Delegation requires trust. It's easier to trust someone if you are completely aligned with them. To ensure alignment, involve your management team in the process of

8: Delegating Authority & Holding People Accountable

determining strategy, setting goals, and identifying action steps. Setting strategy is still the principal's responsibility, but she or he can involve others in the process.

Holding People Accountable

For delegation to be effective there must be accountability. This won't be popular with all employees. Employees love to have responsibility and authority, but not the associated accountability. Unfortunately, if you don't hold employees accountable for results, good outcomes are unlikely to be forthcoming. Achieving meaningful results in any endeavor doesn't happen by itself. It takes dedication, complete focus, and a lot of hard work. If people know they can escape accountability, they are much less likely to make the sacrifices necessary to produce results. In short, delegation of authority without accountability is a recipe for failure.

Accountability is at the core of what makes our capitalist system work. Adam Smith wrote about the "Invisible Hand." Those who work harder, smarter, and produce better results are rewarded for their efforts. This has proven to be a powerful motivator. The world has experience with a system that doesn't reward people for results. According to Karl Marx, this system was predicated on intrinsically motivated people producing according to their ability, and it proposed to reward them according to their need. Thus, the critical link between results and rewards was broken. This system was called communism, and as Eastern Europe discovered in the half-century beyond World War II, it didn't work very well. We learned that, in general, people need rewards that are tightly linked to the results they produce.

Tim was the product manager responsible for the printed circuit board product line. The principal had explained to Tim that his primary responsibility was to ensure that the product line delivered the planned gross margin dollars or more, while not exceeding his marketing budget. First quarter results did not meet expectations. While costs were in line with plan, gross margin dollars were 10 percent behind budget. The miss was the result of both a lower-than-expected gross margin percentage and lower-than-planned sales volume.

The CEO called Tim on the carpet. He asked Tim to explain why his product line had not delivered the gross margin dollars that had been budgeted and what he was planning to do to correct the discrepancy in the second quarter. Unfortunately, his presentation to the CEO took a somewhat different tact. Tim argued that he had done an outstanding job because he had completed all of the tasks that were his responsibility in a timely manner. He cited having completed a new price list that he had delivered on time. He had held training sessions, advertised in trade journals, implemented incentives for the field sales force, and answered their questions accurately.

Tim's argument failed miserably. The CEO's disappointment was undiminished. In fact, he was incensed by Tim's unwillingness to accept responsibility for the shortfall and his lack of responsiveness to the questions. The CEO subsequently determined that Tim was not a good fit for the results-based organization.

When you delegate responsibility to an employee, you must also give them the authority to make the decisions that will impact results. Then you must hold the employee accountable for results, not simply the completion of tasks. To succeed in this endeavor, managers must do several things. First, it is imperative that you and the employee explicitly agree on the goals in advance. It is best if these goals are committed to in writing lest there be subsequent disagreement regarding commitments. It's not fair to hold employees accountable for delivering things that are not clearly stated. While it is desirable that the goals be a stretch, the employee should agree that the results are achievable. If a manager and employee cannot agree on what is achievable, then the manager either has unrealistic expectations or has delegated to the wrong person. Further, it is highly desirable that the goals be quantifiable and objective. For more information on setting appropriate goals, refer to the chapter on developing strategy.

Accountability and authority go hand in hand. There is little in business that is more frustrating to employees than penalizing them for poor results when they didn't have the authority to affect the outcome. Sometimes, this means allowing the accountable employee to make decisions with which you disagree.

Steve was the VP of Sales. Therefore, achieving the sales budget was his responsibility. The CEO thought that the South Central Regional Sales Manager was weak and that Steve should replace him. Steve disagreed. After much debate, the CEO said, "Okay, Steve, you are completely accountable for sales, so it's your call. I've told you what I think, but I'll support whatever you decide to do."

> **If you are going to hold managers accountable, you must give them the authority to make the decisions that have a material impact on their results.**

The South Central Regional Sales Manager remained in place and Steve achieved the sales goal. Had the CEO taken away the VP's authority to choose his own team, Steve would have had an excuse for missing his goals. We're certainly not advocating allowing people to make decisions that will clearly "run the bus into the ditch." However, if a manager has to overrule an employee's decision in order to keep the bus between the lines with any regularity, the wrong person is in that job.

While you should unequivocally hold employees accountable for results, it is also true that you need to view the results in context. A broker/dealer whose revenue was largely a function of the assets under management set goals for the growth of its business in 2008. By the end of the year, an unexpected and nearly unprecedented decline in the Dow had driven assets down dramatically. If you believe, as we do, that it is impossible to predict short-term stock market fluctuations, then you must consider this when judging revenue performance for 2008 versus goal.

However, we also believe that you should only adjust established goals downward with great care. If you lower goals with any frequency, employees who fall behind are likely to spend their time building arguments for having their goals reduced. Instead, businesses would benefit from having their employees devote their energy to finding ways to overcome the shortfall, not justify it. Nevertheless, it is clear that principals must view performance relative to goals in context and make allowances when appropriate.

A Little League baseball coach sat in the first base dugout on a warm summer evening. As he looked on, the batter swung and hit a ground ball to his third baseman. The young infielder, lacking in skills, allowed the ball to roll between his legs and below his glove. The frustrated coach yelled across the field, "Catch the ball, son!"

Was this instruction helpful? Did the coach think that the young man was unaware that he was supposed to catch the ball? Further, was embarrassing the boy in front of his parents, family and friends going to improve the probability that he caught the next ball hit to him? Perhaps a more productive approach would have been to wait for the young man to come back to the dugout between innings and calmly provide him with some coaching on how to field a ground ball. Better yet, the coach could provide the would-be infielder with some additional ground balls at the next practice.

This story, or some version of it, is repeated countless times on Little League fields across the country every evening in the spring and early summer. Unfortunately, those that manage employees are often guilty of the same behaviors. Managers, in an effort to hold employees accountable, often chastise and demoralize their charges when results fall short of expectations. Just as with the Little Leaguer, a far more productive approach is to instruct the underperformer regarding how to do a better job next time. Effective managers often do this by using the Socratic Method. They ask penetrating, open-ended questions. The answers that employees provide allow them to come to their own realizations about how to improve performance. Like Little League coaches, managers who demoralize their employees often do so because they don't know how to coach them to do better. The yelling may assuage the manager's anger, but will do little to improve performance. A much better approach is to coach the employee on how to improve their performance.

Finally, when an employee achieves a goal, take the time to recognize the accomplishment. If accountability only means a stick and never a carrot, your employees won't want it. As we stated in the chapter on managing employees, it is our experience that most people want to be recognized, contributing members of a winning team. So, when results meet or exceed the goal, never miss the opportunity to recognize the accomplishment.

If a principal wants to grow her or his business beyond the size that can be supported by a small business structure, he or she will need to delegate responsibility for tactical decision-making, and hiring and managing workers to others. For the delegation to be successful, hold employees accountable for results, and vest them with the authority to influence those results.

Lessons for Successful Growth

You've decided you want to grow your business, so do it right. Make the commitment to enable your business to grow by delegating tactical decision-making and the hiring and management of workers. But, before delegating, do the proper groundwork:

- Get managers in place who are ready to accept the responsibility that will be delegated to them.

- Develop appropriate process documentation to communicate to the organization how you want things to be done.

- Establish robust metrics so that you can be aware of what is happening in the bowels of the organization without being personally involved.

Once you have delegated the authority to influence results, hold managers accountable. Compare results to goals. When managers come up short, coach them on how to improve their performance.

9: Getting the Right Managers in Place

Continued growth requires delegation, but it's not wise to delegate until the proper managers are in place. To do so could spell disaster. In some ways, this is a reprise to the chapter on getting the right workers in the right jobs. However, there is an important difference. This time the job is more highly leveraged. The stakes are higher. The cost of mistakes will be magnified. An individual production worker can perform poorly and create problems with everything she or he personally touch. But, a manager can cause the entire team for which he or she is responsible to perform poorly. Instead of one employee generating problems, the entire team creates problems. Making the right decision regarding which person to put in each job is even more important when considering management positions.

The first decision you must address when creating a management team is whether to put existing employees into these positions or to bring in people from the outside. This is another difference between hiring workers and hiring managers. When hiring front-line workers, it is usually clear that you will need to bring in people from outside of the organization—there aren't more junior people already in the organization to promote into these roles.

When hiring managers, you must choose between promoting from within and going outside of the organization to recruit talent. It's a make-versus-buy decision and it is often not an easy one. If you decide to promote existing employees, you'll need to develop their management skills. Good managers are not born; they are made. If you decide that you need to look outside of your organization for managers (and almost every company will at some point), you will need to determine how you are going to compete for talent. In the balance of this chapter, we will consider:

- Make-versus-buy – promoting from within or hiring from the outside

- Developing Internal Talent

- Competing for External Talent

Make versus Buy

Gene had earned his high school diploma a few years ago. His first job out of school was working in a warehouse. The warehouse had no heating or cooling. The work was hot in the summer and cold in the winter. Gene had successfully parlayed this initial work experience into a better paying job in a warehouse that was heated and air-conditioned. Gene was a good worker. He was reliable. He arrived on time and worked hard while he was on the job. Both his accuracy and his productivity were good. In fact, management regarded Gene to be the best warehouse employee they had. Further, his coworkers generally liked him.

Then, Gene got his big opportunity. A management position opened up and the company promoted Gene. He received a significant raise. It's true that the best salesperson is not always the best sales manager. Unfortunately, it turns out that the best warehouse worker is not always the best warehouse manager either. Gene was a good employee, but he was out of his depth as a manager. He had no education, training or experience that would have prepared him for a management role. There was no one in the company who could mentor him. He didn't even have a good role model he could emulate.

The company had thrown Gene into the deep end to sink or swim. Sadly, he sank...like a rock. The company provided him with a lot of reports and numbers, but without training, he didn't really understand them. Therefore, he had no basis for good decision-making, which led to poor decisions. His uncertainty showed. His former colleagues liked him as a peer, but didn't respect him as a superior. Things were starting to spiral out of control. Finally, the company demoted Gene and returned him to the warehouse. Accordingly, the company cut his compensation. Unfortunately, Gene was now jaded. His attitude turned sour. A few months later, the company terminated Gene.

The Peter Principle holds that companies tend to promote employees until they ascend into a job that they are not competent to perform. That is, when an employee is performing well in a position, the company promotes them. This will continue until the employee reaches a position where they do not perform well. The reason this happens is that the criteria for promotion in many companies is performance in the current job, not the expectation of strong performance in the job a level up.

Gene is a classic example of the Peter Principle. The company promoted him to his level of incompetence. In many ways, it wasn't his fault. The company promoted a person who did not possess the requisite skill set for success. With significant investment in training, development and coaching, he might have been able to develop such a skill set. Unfortunately, the company did not invest in Gene. In a sense, he was set up to fail.

> **Don't set your employees up for failure by falling victim to the Peter Principle. Only promote an employee when there is a high degree of confidence that he or she can succeed in the new job.**

Please don't misunderstand. We actually have a bias for promoting from within. There are a number of benefits to this practice. It is good for morale. It demonstrates to others that it is possible to advance within the company, which may aid retention. When promoting from within, new managers will enter the role with an understanding of the company that no one from the outside could possess. When existing employees become new managers, the company knows their strengths and weaknesses. By giving existing employees their first opportunity to manage, the cost may be a bit lower when compared to hiring experienced managers from outside the company, at least initially. For the reasons stated above, we do have a bias for promoting from within. However, we also have a bias against setting people up to fail.

Consequently, when filling management positions, a company should ask three questions. First, do we have anyone internally who has the necessary skill set to succeed? Second, if not, do we have anyone who could develop the requisite skill set with appropriate investment? Finally, could this person develop the skill set in a timeframe that would make it reasonable to promote him or her now? If the answers to these questions do not yield a good internal candidate, you should look outside the organization for management talent.

The answers to these questions may not always be clear, even after the fact. We interviewed a great company, which offered a fantastic service and had a clear mission. The principal was passionate about the work and the value it brought to her customers. She was a true visionary—concentrating her efforts on the next steps for the business. She had grown the company to a midsize structure. It had become a multi-million dollar enterprise with more than 100 employees in just over five years. Her first employee was still with her and had grown with the company assuming the role of chief financial officer with responsibility for a very large portion of the business.

During our interview, this obviously bright and energetic man made several comments about his managers. However, one comment stood out. "I told my managers that they need to have their staff meetings and then report the results to me. I don't need to be in their staff meetings running things." We started to wonder about the CFO's ability to delegate and the quality of his managers. Had he promoted them from within? What were their backgrounds? Did they have the skills to be managers, or were they better suited to be great followers and doers?

We also started wondering about the CFO. He must be a competent manager to have successfully grown the business as he had, but was he doing a good job of selecting the managers who worked for him? As the business continues on its path, it will need ever-increasing levels of talent to survive and flourish. Will this CFO be able to recognize and either grow or recruit the horsepower necessary to get the business to the next level?

This can be a tough call. Especially when the people who helped the company mature from its infancy no longer have the skill set or talent needed to lead or sometimes even to work in the business as it grows and changes. Tom Winfree, the CEO of Village Bank, points out that, "The people you need to start with are not necessarily the people you need when you grow." Jacques Moore of Moore Cadillac echoes Tom's sentiment when he says, "You don't have to play the hand you are dealt. You can put cards back and get new ones. You can change your team." Yes, it's doable, but it's not always easy. During our research, we spoke with several companies who struggled with this issue:

- An organization that needed to automate to survive could not let go of the employees who were essential when it had performed work manually—even though the employees did not have the skills needed to succeed in the new business model. The employees struggled and so did the business, causing great stress to the individuals and the organization as a whole. In this case, the CEO was not able to make the emotional decision to terminate the employees who had worked at the company since its inception. The full impact remains to be seen.

- Another company, which started with three principals, decided to leave one of the principals in a lower-level role after determining he did not have the skills needed to lead the company as it grew. In this case, the principal who remained at the lower level in the organization became a strong and valued player while the other principals assumed roles as the chief executive officer and chief marketing officer. While this was a painful decision, it has so far proved to be an effective one.

- In a very unusual case, the principal of a midsized company recognized that his skills were in sales and not in running a growing midsize company. He hired an experienced professional manager to be the president and run the business on his behalf. The owner continued to support the business in a sales role, but left the management of the business to the new president. The company continued to grow and prosper under the guidance of the new leader. Not many business owners could let go to this degree in order for their enterprise to continue to grow, but in this case, it worked well.

One of the hardest parts of letting go for most principals has to do with their people. It is easier to let go of processes that no longer help your business, to let go of tasks that are no longer appropriate, but to let go of people—that takes a special will and determination to grow and survive. This is particularly true since most entrepreneurs who successfully start and grow businesses care deeply about their people.

It comes down to a make-versus-buy decision. Can you, and would it be expedient to, grow the people you have into new roles as your business expands and changes or will you have to look outside the organization for the skills, talent and experience needed to take your organization to the next level? How does one decide, especially when there is a heartfelt attachment to the existing employees and sometimes a family or friend connection involved? Can you remove the emotional roadblocks and look at the situation pragmatically? To successfully grow, the principal will have to let go— sometimes that may mean letting go of good people who simply cannot grow with the organization.

Developing Internal Talent

In spite of his long hours and hard work, John's small business was struggling. There always seemed to be cash flow issues. Frequently, there was barely enough money to make payroll. Oh, he paid his suppliers, but often not on time. One night, late as usual, John thought he would try to endear himself to his wife by bringing home Chinese takeout for dinner from the shop next door. He walked over and ordered moo shoo pork with fried rice. "It'll be

Walking back through the door to his office, John thought, if I go to my desk, I'll just get involved in something and forget about dinner. Exhausted, he plopped himself down at his office manager's desk. Becky had been with John for several years and managed the books as well as the office. He trusted her completely. As he relaxed, he started staring at the paperwork lying on her desk. Then he noticed something that didn't look right. Curious, he began to dig deeper. A few minutes later when he left to get the Chinese takeout order, he had the company's books tucked under his arm.

That night, John didn't sleep. Instead, he sat at his kitchen table and poured over the books. By morning, he was convinced. Becky had been embezzling from the company for quite some time. The next morning John confronted her with his discovery of the prior evening. When faced with the evidence, she confessed and was terminated. Becky agreed to pay the money back. John agreed not to press charges. It was a very sad day for all concerned.

You'd think that the story would end here. Unfortunately, it doesn't. One of the current employees took over the duties of the office manager. Several months passed. The person handling the accounts was having trouble getting the books to balance. In frustration, John called Becky and hired her back!

A few months later, Becky came to John to ask for a loan. In-depth questioning revealed that she had surreptitiously "borrowed" some money from a local youth sports organization where she was the treasurer. She'd done it again! This brought a permanent end to her employment at John's company. By the way, John did not give her the loan. (We have changed the names, but this story is true— we swear, you couldn't make up this stuff.) Clearly, if the employee assuming the duties of the office manager had been properly trained, there would have been no need to rehire a woman who had previously embezzled from the company. Even if there was no one in the organization capable of training her, an external trainer could have been hired—a missed opportunity.

Let Go To Grow

If you want to promote from within you need a group of people that have the appropriate skill sets waiting in the wings. This won't happen by accident. It requires hiring junior people that have the intellectual horsepower and the behaviors that you want in a manager. You will then need to develop and mentor these people so that they will be ready for the challenge of being a manager when the opportunity presents itself. This model has been successful. For example, McKinsey & Company, one of the preeminent management-consulting firms in the world, fills the senior ranks almost exclusively from within. To do this, they continuously hire graduates of the top-tier business schools who have the potential to grow into more senior roles with time, experience, and training.

After you have hired people with management potential, you will need to develop them. In part, you should accomplish this through formal training programs. In addition, it is a good idea to provide management opportunities ahead of promotion into a management role. This may take the form of allowing the person you are grooming for management to lead a taskforce or other project. For example, one of our clients identified a young woman whom the president believes has the potential to become an excellent manager. To help the high-potential employee gain management experience, the company has asked her to lead a team of several people. This team's goal is to grow the sales of a particular product line. Further, the company hired an executive coach to help the young woman develop the skills she needs to succeed in the role.

One small business owner had built quite a nice life for himself and his family. He explained, "My house is paid for, my cars are paid for, my house at the river is paid for, my boat is paid for, my jet skis are paid for, and the building that houses my business is paid for." When asked about his long-term goals he explained that he planned to step out of the day-to-day running of the business and let his son, who was an employee, assume the top job one day. He said that the rent he would charge his son for the building where the business was located would be his retirement income.

The only potential flaw in this plan would be if his son failed to continue to operate the business successfully. When asked what he

> **If you want to be able to promote from within, you must develop your people before you need them.**

was doing to prepare his son for this role he explained, "Each year I take a longer vacation." The comment was humorous, but it was also accurate. He was grooming his son to run the business by allowing him to assume the leadership role while he was out of the office. He then spent time coaching his son regarding the proper way to manage the enterprise. The owner was spending more and more time out of the office to allow his son to gain experience running the company, years before he would have to fly solo.

Promoting managers from within can be a successful strategy, but success is not guaranteed. You will need to plan and work towards it. It won't happen automatically. It requires hiring people with the right core skill set (i.e., intellectual horsepower and behaviors). Once you hire them, you will need to develop and mentor them so they will be ready when the opportunity presents itself.

A company that wants to promote from within will also need to develop proactive plans to retain these employees. You can't afford to lose those you have groomed for senior roles. A very real risk is that after the company invests time, effort, and money to get an employee ready for a more senior role, the employee finds an opportunity outside of the company before there is an opening internally. Timing is important. When an employee is ready for more responsibility, you need to find them an opportunity fairly quickly.

When trying to fill a senior position, even if the successful candidate ultimately comes from outside of the organization, there is a benefit to considering internal candidates. We know a very successful senior human resources executive who asserts that companies should post all jobs internally. This is a good practice even if management believes strongly that there are no acceptable candidates inside the organization. She explains,

Management may not think that there are any qualified internal candidates. That doesn't mean that there aren't people who believe they are qualified and who would like to be considered. If these people don't have a chance to apply for the job, they will likely feel hard done by and be resentful of management. If unqualified internal candidates apply for the job, it provides an opportunity for management to coach the applicant regarding what they would need to do to be qualified for the job. Most people appreciate the company considering them and receiving coaching so that they can be successful when applying for future positions. The cost of the internal posting process is small when compared to the benefit of improved employee morale.

Competing for External Talent

While we do have a bias for internal promotion, there are also advantages to going outside of your firm and there are times when it is unequivocally the right thing to do. Outsiders can bring skills that your firm needs but does not currently possess. Jim Snyder is the Chairman and CEO of Odell an architectural design firm. When he decided that he wanted to take his firm to the next level, he went outside. He found a partner in Roger Soto, a designer who is recognized worldwide for his expertise. According to Jim, "Within 12 months Roger had reshaped our firm."

Hiring talent can be faster than growing your own and in certain circumstances may require less training and development expense. Consequently, if you have an immediate need and no insiders that are ready to accept the challenge, this is likely the way to go. Outsiders will not be indoctrinated with how things have always been done. They will likely bring some fresh thinking and new ideas.

One caution when comparing internal candidates to external prospects is that you will know the internal candidates well. Therefore, you will know their faults. The external candidates will do everything possible to keep you from seeing theirs until after you have hired them. When making a decision between an internal and an external candidate, make sure to include these facts in the calculus that results in a hiring decision.

After careful consideration, you've reached the difficult decision that you do not have the internal talent you need to fill the open management position at the present time. You are going to have to look outside of your organization for management talent. The process of hiring a manager is the same as that which we explained in the chapter on getting the right people in the right jobs. You have to (1) know what you need, (2) understand what you have to offer, (3) cast a broad net with a narrow focus, (4) leverage multiple methods and opinions, and (5) trust, but verify.

Of course, you are going to want to get the best people that you can attract. The advice to hire great people into management roles is obvious. Who could argue? What baseball coach wouldn't want to have Derek Jeter playing shortstop? It's a no-brainer. You want stars in key roles, but what if you're not the New York Yankees with millions backing you?

If you are hiring the executive leadership team of a Fortune 500 company, you can afford to be very choosy. Individuals from top-tier schools with exceptional credentials, track records and experience are likely to apply. Large companies attract talent by offering exceptional salaries and bonuses, long-term compensation packages loaded with stock options, and the chance to work in highly visible organizations. Unfortunately, when you are a small or midsize company with limited resources, your chance of hiring these individuals is slim.

As pointed out previously, achieving clarity regarding what you need and want in each role is a critical first step. Having accomplished this, you know what you would like to find. It would be nice to be able to employ your dream candidate, but the reality is, you will likely have to compromise.

Consider the example of the Oakland Athletics, a mid-market

baseball team that plays in the same league as the New York Yankees, the Boston Red Sox, the Texas Rangers, and the Los Angeles Angels. In a sport where money buys talent and large markets mean a lot of money, how could the Oakland A's hope to compete? Billy Beane, the team's general manager, faced a daunting challenge. In describing it, Michael Lewis, the author of *Money Ball* writes:

> *There was no simple way to approach the problem that Billy Beane was trying to solve. It read like an extra credit question on an algebra quiz: You have $40 million to spend on twenty-five baseball players. Your opponent has already spent $126 million on its own 25 players, and holds perhaps another $100 million in reserve. What do you do with your forty million to avoid humiliating defeat? "What you don't do," said Billy, "is what the Yankees do. If we do what the Yankees do, we lose every time, because they're doing it with three times more money than we are." A poor team couldn't afford to go out shopping for big league stars in the prime of their careers.*

Surprisingly, the Oakland A's, with the second lowest payroll in baseball won 91 games in 2000, while losing only 71. They improved in 2001 winning an astonishing 102 games, while losing only 60. How did they accomplish this? In part, they did it by identifying characteristics that were important to them and predicted success in their organization that their better-heeled competitors weren't looking for.

For example, one thing that is very difficult to predict in baseball is how well a good hitter at the college level will perform in the major leagues. Sometimes good college hitters are a real flop in the majors. The A's figured out that one of the most important statistics when trying to predict success of a good college hitter in the majors is the number of walks received at the college level. It turns out that the more walks a good hitter gets in college; the more likely he is to be a good hitter in the majors. That seems a bit odd. Why is the number of walks a good hitter gets in college a predictor of his performance in the major leagues? Good hitters are supposed to hit, not walk.

Actually, there is a fairly straightforward reason. College players that walk a lot don't swing at bad pitches. In college the pitchers aren't as good as they are in the major league. Even if you swing at bad pitches in college, pitchers make mistakes. You will get enough good pitches that you can still be a successful hitter. However, in the majors the pitchers are able to locate their pitches much more accurately. If you will swing at bad pitches, that's all you'll see. Unfortunately, you can't be a good hitter if all you see is bad pitches at which you swing.

> **When recruiting talent from outside of your organization:**
> - **Identify exactly what you need**
> - **Understand what you have to offer**
> - **Cast a broad net with a narrow focus**
> - **Leverage multiple methods and opinions**
> - **Trust, but verify.**

The Oakland A's were able to be successful because they knew what they were looking for and it was different from what the big dogs were trying to find. Small and midsize businesses have to play the same game. The best way to do this is by compromising on education and experience, but insisting on hiring smart people with the behaviors you want.

The big dogs will be looking for Ivy League undergraduates, MBAs from top-tier schools and lengthy track records with prestigious companies, and they will get them. Midsize companies may not be able to hire people with these credentials, but they can hire smart people, with a great work ethic and good people skills whose education and experience is somewhat more modest. Like the Oakland A's competing with the New York Yankees, to win you have to zig when they zag. Compromise on education and experience, but don't settle when it comes to intellectual horsepower and desired behavior.

Further, the entrepreneurial environment of smaller businesses and the variety and responsibility that comes from wearing many hats is very appealing to some managers. The ability to take a process from start to finish rather than only performing a small piece of a job is often unique to the small-business environment.

For example, we know a gifted human resources professional who interviewed successfully with a Fortune 200 company. She was also considering employment opportunities with smaller firms. The compensation and benefits at the large company were significantly better than those offered by the other companies she was considering.

At the smaller business, she would be the head of human resources. She would be responsible for a broad set of functions ranging from hiring to compliance to consulting with senior management. She would be a part of the senior management team that set strategy, policy and direction for the entire business. At the Fortune 200 company she would toil in only one very narrowly focused area of human resources. In the end, the professional challenge of having broader job responsibilities outweighed the better compensation and benefits. She chose to work with a smaller company.

When a company grows to midsize, the principal must delegate people management and tactical decision-making or see the growth of the enterprise stagnate. Worse than not delegating is delegating to employees who are not ready to accept the responsibility. Getting the proper managers in place is a prerequisite to effective delegation. While assembling a good management team can be challenging, it is doable if you follow the steps outlined above.

Lessons for Successful Growth

Ensure that you have the right managers in place so that you can delegate tactical decision-making and management responsibilities to them. To do this:

- Determine whether you will make or buy the management talent that you need—be willing to make tough decisions when necessary.

- If you decide to pursue a policy of developing talent internally, begin the process well before the need presents itself.

- If you are going to look outside of your organization for management talent, decide how you are going to compete with the big dogs to get the caliber of person you need.

10: Establishing Systems and Documenting Processes

We worked with a family-owned broker/dealer—a company that executes trades in the financial markets on behalf of its network of financial representatives. The family placed almost exclusive emphasis on sales and marketing. As a result, the business grew. The enterprise began as a micro business operated by the founder and his wife. Now, run by the second generation, it had grown to a midsize business serving about 450 financial representatives across the US.

Because the owners had little interest in operations, they delegated this responsibility to a series of managers over the years. The managers never invested the time to develop appropriate systems and establish well-documented processes. Operations floundered. There was little written information regarding how the employees should perform their work. What was written down had fallen into disuse and, therefore, didn't match actual practice.

Most of the knowledge about how to do things resided in the heads of the experienced processors. It became "tribal knowledge" as processors passed down work instructions through an oral tradition. Those processors who had worked there the longest had the most knowledge and became the "tribal elders." Because processes weren't systematically written down, there was no basis for formal training. It was all OJT (on-the-job training). Tribal elders passed down knowledge regarding how to execute the work to new hires. Unfortunately, this method of knowledge transfer is less than reliable.

Remember the game many of us played in grade school where the teacher whispered something to the first student in the class. Each student quietly passed the message on to the next through the entire class. When the final student shared with the class what she or he had heard, it bore little resemblance to what the teacher had originally said. Passing information from tribal elder to new hire about how to do a job works no better. As with any oral tradition, over time information is lost, processes are changed, and inconsistency occurs.

The back-office work of a broker/dealer is extremely nuanced. Precision is critical. As would be expected, the lack of written processes resulted in inconsistencies. Some tribal elders did things one way. Others did the same thing in a different way. The tribal knowledge was inconsistent. With the best intentions in the world, the tribal elders passed on these inconsistencies to the people they trained and at each step little things were inadvertently left out or changed slightly. The result was that employees could process a particular piece of work in a number of different ways with unequal results.

For example, depending on who processed a particular trade, and how they had been taught to execute the work, it might settle in one day or in three days. Imagine the frustration that investors felt when they recognized that the same type of trade took different amounts of time to settle. From their perspective, the process seemed quite random and in many ways, it was.

The lack of clear process also resulted in uncertainty regarding how employees should execute the work. Processors had no documentation to consult when they had questions. They could not be certain how to proceed. Therefore, processors were often left to do what they thought was right. As you can imagine, this resulted in frequent processing errors. The financial representatives were often livid. Clients were unhappy. The broker/dealer incurred significant expense to correct its errors and make clients whole. The situation was bad in normal times, but unprecedented market volatility in 2008 and 2009 led to a doubling of processing volume in a very short period. Because of the lack of consistent, documented processes, the result was near catastrophe.

Properly documented processes can prevent such problems by ensuring that employees complete work in the same way regardless of who does it or when it is done. Astyra, a technology-staffing firm, has developed hundreds of documented processes over the years. President Sam Young said, "Since we have stepped back, people do follow the processes." This consistency ensures that employees complete their work in the way the principals want every time.

> **Once an organization reaches midsize, it requires documented process to communicate to the organization how to execute specific tasks.**

When a company has a small business structure, the principal is close to the operation. There are relatively few employees. Those employees continuously interact with the principal and with each other. The principal can easily communicate processes to the entire organization and is always there to ensure consistency.

The owner of a business that imports electronic components for resale to American manufacturers employs several people. There is a man who operates the warehouse. Three women work in the office—ordering product, managing inventory, answering the phones, sending invoices, collecting receivables and keeping the books. The owner does most of the selling himself. He knows exactly what each person is doing and how the work is progressing. He has trained every employee personally, explaining exactly how he wants things done and he checks behind his employees to make sure they do things his way. There is little process documentation. There doesn't need to be. The principal is able to enforce consistent process because he remains involved in every detail of the work.

In such an environment, an oral tradition can work just fine. Even without formal documentation, employees complete the work in a consistent manner because the principal is there to ensure that they do. Of course, as the enterprise grows, the principal will not be as involved in the day-to-day operation of the business. He or she will have delegated decision-making. No one person will have both detailed knowledge of the entire enterprise and day-to-day interaction with every process. Communication between employees responsible for executing the primary work of the business will be less consistent. Without formal processes, things will break down as they did at the broker/dealer described above. To avoid this situation, as your company grows to midsize, you must take the time to clarify your processes. Then once you are clear about how you want things done, you must document your processes—committing them to writing is a step that you cannot skip.

Good process documentation allows principals to communicate to employees how they want things done and to ensure that work gets done consistently across the organization and over time. But, there are other important reasons to invest in robust process documentation.

When good process documentation exists, it lessens the impact of key employees leaving the organization. We worked with one company in which the principal could not bring himself to make a needed personnel change, in large part because the problem employee was considered irreplaceable. She had a lot of detailed information in her head about how the company functioned that would have been lost if she were no longer an employee. If the company had well documented processes, it could have terminated the problem employee with minimal impact to the company.

Mark Creery is the president of Data Directions, a software development company. To protect key employees from being "hit by the proverbial bus," Mark insists that his employees thoroughly document all processes. He tells them to "Document like they won't be showing up tomorrow."

Good process documentation also serves as the basis for training employees to do tasks that are new to them. The documentation ensures that the trainer presents the same information every time.

It also acts as a record newly trained employees can refer to if they have questions about how to do things.

Finally, well-documented processes provide a basis from which to improve. If employees execute work inconsistently, it is very difficult to implement consistent changes to the way they do things across the organization. Conversely, if the organization has good process documentation and the employees follow it, making changes to the way they do things is considerably easier.

Developing well-documented processes can be a significant undertaking. This is especially true if the company has grown to a size where it should have previously documented processes and things have gotten somewhat out of control. Beth Bailey is the president of The Pediatric Connection, a company that provides home healthcare for children. She says that developing and maintaining effectively documented processes is "tedious, cumbersome, and difficult, but you need them." It requires a focused and concerted effort on an ongoing basis, but difficult or not, it's a necessary undertaking. The good news is that, in our experience, the rewards are worth the cost.

Benefits of good documentation:
1. **Ensures that work is done consistently**
2. **Lessens the impact of key employees leaving**
3. **Makes training workers more efficient and effective**
4. **Provides a basis from which to make improvements**

Don't get us wrong. We are not bureaucrats. We are not advocating creating unnecessary paperwork. We completely understand that this may seem like non-value added work. No customer is going to pay you more because you have good process documentation. At the same time, in our experience, failure to establish appropriate process documentation as a business grows is a recipe for disaster that will result in inconsistent quality, the inability to deliver products and services in a timely manner, and cost overruns. This will result in unhappy customers, and frustrated employees.

In addition, you, as the principal, will not be able to ensure that the work of your organization gets done the way you want—every time. You will constantly need to check behind your people's work. There are not enough hours in the day or days in the week for you to accomplish this. In the long run, good process documentation will have an extremely positive impact on a company's bottom line and the principal's sanity.

To be sure, this is nontrivial work, but adherence to the following guidelines will ensure that the work goes smoothly:

- Identify the systems and processes to be documented

- Choose the right person to oversee the documentation

- Ensure that the documentation matches the actual work

- Require that process documentation be a living record

- Ensure continuous improvement

Identify Processes to be Documented

There are a large number of processes in every company. For example, every product that a manufacturing company produces requires a process to build. Pulling a part out of inventory, packing it, and shipping it is a process. Executing a stock trade is a process. When a direct mail company sends out a solicitation, it requires a process. There are also processes associated with hiring employees, developing a budget, and executing employee performance evaluations. So, which of these processes should you document? The short answer is all of them.

More specifically, in a midsize company, you should document any activity that has the following characteristics:

- **You repeat the activity** – One-off activities do not need to be documented. Pragmatically, there would be little reason for documentation other than, perhaps, to provide a historic record of proceedings.

- **It is important that employees execute the activity consistently across the organization and over time** – If multiple people across the organization perform the activity and it is important that they all execute in the same way, documentation will be helpful. Similarly, if employees need to perform the activity consistently from one day, week, month, or year to the next, documenting the activity will help to ensure consistency.

- **It is important that organizational memory remain intact** – If only one person knows how to perform a particular function and that person gets hit by the proverbial bus (or is lured away by a competitor), you will lose institutional knowledge. Those people left in the company will have to recreate the processes from scratch. Your organization will waste time and will most likely experience more errors. Proper documentation can prevent this.

- **There is a frequent need to train people to do the particular activity** – Process documentation is an extremely useful training tool. It ensures that the trainer is both consistent and thorough. The instructor won't inadvertently leave items out of the training. It also serves as a reference manual for the trainees and will help them remember what the instructor taught.

Pragmatically, a company may not have the resources to undertake documentation of all its processes at once. The project will need to be phased and will take time. But, that's not a good excuse for delaying the start of this important work. Prioritize and get on with it. The old Chinese proverb is correct: "The journey of a thousand miles begins with a single step."

In determining which processes to document first, it is important to begin by developing a comprehensive list of the processes you want to document across the entire business. Remember that you can most assuredly document some processes in parallel. For example, while Operations is documenting how they build a widget, Finance can be working on the budgeting process, and

10: Establishing Systems & Documenting Processes

Human Resources can be outlining the performance management process. Because these efforts involve different departments, they should not be mutually exclusive, and therefore, can happen at the same time.

However, it is likely that you will need to document some processes in series. This will be the case either because you will need to know the details of one process before you can establish another process, or because documenting the two processes will require the same limited resources. When you must know the details of one process before you can begin work documenting a second process, it is clear which you should do first. When documenting two separate processes requires the same limited resource, you must determine a priority order.

Assign higher priority to those activities that will have the most impact on the customer. In general, internally focused processes can receive lower priority. Even if a process will impact customers, processes with issues should receive a higher priority than those that are currently running smoothly. For example, if a widget manufacturer is experiencing quality issues due to inconsistent manufacturing processes, this may well be the first place to start with documentation. On the other hand, if the widget manufacturer is having no issues producing widgets of acceptable quality, in a timely manner, and at a good cost, widget production may not be the first process to document. Make sure you are getting the biggest bang for your buck.

First, identify the processes you need to document and then prioritize them appropriately.

A second factor to consider when determining which process to document first is how often people are trained in the process. You should document frequently taught processes first. The most important point is to get the documentation project started. Process documentation is very important, but there will always be something more urgent. Successful businesses don't ignore the urgent, but they make time for the important.

Choose the Right Person to Lead Documentation

Top management will need to support the documentation process if it is to be successful. Further, this support must be highly visible. It isn't enough for senior management to tell a small group of people behind closed doors that they are supportive. The whole organization must be aware of the importance that senior management places on the initiative. It is highly likely that the person charged with process documentation will have to get significant help from a large number of people who do not report to him or her. People who are busy and have other jobs to do will only provide this support if they understand it is a priority for senior management.

There is huge benefit to having a single person responsible for the documentation process. Point accountability is critical to the ultimate success of the effort. This person need not actually write the documentation for every process. However, he or she will be ultimately responsible for the quality and consistency of the work. Obviously, the person entrusted with this responsibility must be a good writer, but they also need to be a very structured thinker. They must be able to write clear and concise process descriptions.

While point accountability is critical, this person should not lock himself or herself in an office and craft the documentation in isolation. Ultimately, the subject matter experts (SMEs) must have input. These are the people who are doing the work and who really know what is going on. There are numerous ways to accomplish this. The person responsible for documentation can interview the SME, develop a draft, and have the SME review it for accuracy. Alternatively, the SME could develop the first draft. In either case, the SME must be integrally involved in the process.

Do not construct the documentation by simply asking management about the process. We worked with a company that was pursuing its ISO 9000 certification. This certification requires that a company document all of its important processes and that the documentation matches the actual work. The person charged with developing the documentation sat with each of the managers and they jointly developed the ISO 9000 documentation.

When the auditors arrived, the company failed to receive the certification it sought. The problem was that when the auditor interviewed the people who were actually doing the work, they discovered that, in many cases, the documentation didn't match the actual processes. The managers had a general idea of how employees executed the work, but they didn't have the details right. When the company got the employees who were actually doing the work involved in reworking the documentation to reflect actual practice, it received certification.

As with any important task, point accountability is crucial.

Document the activity that is actually happening, not what management thinks is happening. These are unequivocally not always the same. If you wish to change the way employees complete the work after you document the process, you can absolutely do that. Of course, it's important to make sure that both the documentation and the way employees do things actually change in tandem.

Documentation Must Match Actual Work

Alpha Industries invested many hours in documenting its processes. After completing the documentation, it was saved in very organized electronic files. Unfortunately, there it sat. The only time anyone accessed the documentation was when a problem surfaced. What was actually done was compared with what the documentation said should have been done. Most of the time, the result of the investigation was disappointing. The way employees had processed the work didn't match the documentation. The employees who processed the work didn't have easy access to the documented procedures. In addition, management did not hold them accountable for following those procedures. There was no linkage between the documented processes and the actual work. When actual execution didn't match the stated processes, it left the company liable for losses.

A company in a heavily regulated industry was required to have process documentation on hand for the regulators to review, and this they did faithfully. When asked if the employees who actually did the work had access to this documentation, the principal, quite honestly, said yes. He explained that the documentation is in a notebook in the supervisor's office and any employee could review it at any time. Then we asked the supervisor how often employees actually reviewed the documentation. The answer was essentially never. It's nice to have process documentation, but if the way the employees do the work is to bear any resemblance to the words written on a page, there must be a very tight linkage between the two. It won't happen by accident.

> **To be effective, the people doing the work must use the process documentation and you must hold them accountable for doing their work as specified.**

Too often, companies invest a lot of time and effort to develop process documentation that then lies buried in an electronic file or sits on a shelf in a manager's office collecting dust. When this happens, "process drift" will occur. That is, the way the work gets done will morph over time. At some point, the documentation will no longer match actual practice. Although this may meet some regulatory requirement, it destroys value. Aside from being a colossal waste of time, it's extremely frustrating to those who spent the time and effort developing the documentation. Further, it's a huge missed opportunity because all of the value the process documentation could have produced is lost. To be useful, management must communicate the documentation to the people who are actually doing the work, and it must be easily accessible to them. Employees should refer to it frequently and be held accountable for conducting their work as prescribed in the documentation.

To avoid process drift, you should perform routine audits to ensure that the documentation reflects the way employees execute the work. Some companies will choose to audit only a few processes each week. The audit then becomes an ongoing, never-ending effort. These companies think this makes the audit process less burdensome. To ensure the audits are objective, they should be performed by employees from outside the department responsible for maintaining the documentation. In an ideal world, people from outside the company would perform the audit.

Be a Living Record

Alpha Industries, described above, faced another problem when the documentation was buried in electronic files. Because employees didn't regularly use the documentation, it was forgotten. Therefore, when actual processes changed, they didn't update the documentation. This served to exacerbate the differences between the documented processes and the way employees performed the work.

Obviously, the world of business is not static. Circumstances change and organizations must alter their processes in response. People discover better ways to get their work done. Processes need to morph to take advantage of opportunities and to avoid adverse consequences. That's fine. Documenting a process doesn't mean that it is cast in stone. You can improve your processes in any way that is appropriate, but you must reflect this new reality in the documentation.

Further, there needs to be a designated person whose job it is to oversee the changes to any specific piece of documentation. It may sound strange, but there should be a process to change the process.

The person responsible for managing the process changes may need to get approval from one or more other people before he or she implements the process change, but there should be a single person responsible for overseeing the process documentation. Documentation must be a set of living documents that continuously change to mirror evolving processes. Because of this, it is important to keep track of changes as they occur—version control will be critical.

Ensure Continuous Improvement

Until now we have focused entirely on making sure the documentation matches the way employees perform the actual work. While this is an important first step, there has been no discussion of how to go about improving processes. Once you have documented your processes and you have a stable operation, you have a basis from which to begin continuous improvement. Dr. W. Edwards Deming, a well-recognized expert in process improvement, indicated that, depending on the business, between 80 and 95 percent of problems are process driven. Ignoring the need for process improvement in your business is to condemn yourself to a frustrating life consumed with rushing from issue to issue putting out fires. Avoid this by seizing the opportunity to improve your processes continuously. We will focus on two types of process improvement: (1) Quality Improvement, and (2) Cycle Time Reduction.

> **When you identify better ways to do the work, you must change the process documentation to reflect the new reality.**

- Quality – An executive walks into a quality seminar. Sitting on the table in front of him is a rectangular cake pan with sides that are about 2-inches tall. The pan is half filled with ¼-inch diameter beads. About half of the beads are red and half are white.

There is a thin, rectangular paddle lying on the table beside the pan. The paddle fits nicely inside the cake pan with a bit of room to spare on each side. One hundred evenly spaced holes have been drilled in the paddle. The holes are just less than ¼-inch in diameter so that the beads will sit in the holes, but not fall through.

The instructor tells the executive that this is a production process. As the operator, he has to slide the paddle into the pan underneath the beads. Then he must raise the paddle slowly so that one bead rests in each hole and the other beads fall back into the pan. The instructor also explains that he has to capture only white beads. Any hole that contains a red bead is considered an error.

When the executive executes the process, to no one's surprise, about half of the holes contain a white bead and about half contain a red bead. The executive repeats the process several times with similar unhappy, albeit predictable, results. The instructor then explains that management is very concerned about the quality problems with his work. Therefore, they are instituting an incentive compensation program. The executive will receive a $100 bill each time he removes only white beads. After several additional attempts, he is no richer. At this point, the instructor tells the executive that his quality continues to be unacceptable and that management has decided to terminate him immediately. A replacement is hired, but his results are approximately the same as those of the now terminated executive.

In this little game, the employees followed the process specified by management. The process inherently yielded errors. Incentive compensation can improve how well employees follow a process, but if the operator is already compliant, it won't change results. Even threatening employees with termination or replacement won't help. The obvious point of this exercise is that when the process inherently produces errors, to get better quality, you must improve the process.

Many people have tried to help businesses improve quality. You may know many of their names. These gurus have been with us for quite a while. In 1946, at the conclusion of World War II, the War Department sent Dr. W. Edwards Deming to Japan to help with the rebuilding effort. There he introduced the notion of statistical process control. While his ideas are completely valid, for most small to midsize businesses they are the rough equivalent of killing a fly with a nuclear bomb. It'll work, but the cost may well exceed the benefit.

In the early 1980s, quality guru Phil Crosby taught us that quality is free. At the time, there was a general perception that to improve quality, a company had to spend money. High quality equals high cost. To be sure, there are clearly situations where spending money will help to improve quality. For example, replacing an old machine with one that is state-of-the-art can often help to improve quality. However, Crosby's point was that if you consider the true cost of poor quality (e.g., rework, scrap, waste, unhappy customers, etc.), the benefit of improving quality almost always exceeds the cost. Crosby wrote eloquently on the topic. He did an outstanding job of marketing quality.

Add to these names the likes of Joseph Juran, Walter Shewhart, and the list of "quality gurus" goes on. In addition to these pioneers, there is a long list of quality programs. These include Six Sigma, ISO 9000, Total Quality Management, SAS-70 and so on. The business world is full of quality experts and quality programs, but for most small to midsize businesses, an extensive quality program utilizing higher-level mathematics is not going to be the solution to their issues. Rather, what they need is a down-to-earth, common-sense approach to quality as outlined in the following steps:

o **Document your processes** – For small and midsized businesses to improve quality, processes must be consistent across the organization and over time. Things must be done the same way every time. If the organization has reached midsize or larger, it can only accomplish this when it has well-documented processes.

- ○ **Identify quality issues** – A company named Rehrig produced large quantities of shopping carts. The plastic baskets sat in nickel-chrome plated chassis. Rehrig was diligent about measuring quality and held each department accountable for their scrap rates. Unknown to anyone, the roof of the warehouse sprung a leak. Rainwater dripped onto the tubing that was to form the chassis. Over time, some of the tubing rusted. The warehouse workers saw the rust but didn't report it because they didn't want the scrap or rework charged to their department.

In the bending department, the operators saw the rust as well, but for the same reason didn't report it. Neither the welding department nor the plating department reported the rust. Instead, they passed along the problem. Happily, scrap rates remained low in all departments. By the time the nickel-chrome plated chassis reached the assembly department, shiny metal covered the rust. The problem was no longer visible. Employees assembled and fitted the tubing with plastic baskets and wheels to complete the process. The carts then passed final inspection and were shipped to customers. Unfortunately, because the chassis were rusty, the nickel-chrome plating soon started to pop off. Customers were unhappy and returned many of the carts.

If employees had reported the rusty tubing in the warehouse before the company added any value, the cost would have been nominal. Sandblasting would have easily removed the rust. However, because the process penalized the department that identified scrap, the problem went unre-ported. By the time the company discovered the quality issue, it was very expensive indeed. Customers were upset; the company had to pay shipping costs in both directions; and the company had added significant value to the metal tubing that it now had to throw out. Although it could reuse some of the cart parts, the rework was expensive. The problem is obvious.

This story illustrates the 1-10-100 rule. If a problem is identified and corrected at the point of occurrence, the cost will be a magnitude of 1. If the quality problem works its way through the process, but the company catches it before reaching the customer, the cost will be a magnitude of 10. However, if the problem reaches the customer, the cost will be a magnitude of 100. Clearly, there is benefit to identifying quality problems as quickly as possible.

Employees and management must embrace quality issues as opportunities to improve. Management must take extra care not to "shoot the messenger." No company wants to discover that quality issues exist in its processes. However, companies must view raising the issues that do exist as a positive thing. They should not sweep them under the carpet. Companies are all too often surprised when they routinely chastise people who raise quality concerns and then find that people hide these issues. Companies should reward employees who identify quality issues, not punish them.

o **Fix the problem for the customer** – The steak was well-done. There was no doubt, but medium was what had been ordered. The waiter asked if the temperature was correct. It wasn't. He apologized profusely and immediately whisked the plate back to the kitchen. In a few short moments the manager appeared. She apologized again and informed us that we would have a new steak in just a few minutes. As the manager left, a waiter delivered a perfect steak to our table.

When the dishes were cleared, the manager appeared again, and this time with a dessert tray. She invited us to choose something nice, on the house. When the check arrived, both the steak and the dessert were gratis. When the manager returned our credit card, she also brought a $25 gift certificate. She hoped that we would give her restaurant another chance. She assured us that the next time they would get the temperature right. We left happier than we might have been if the steak had been prepared correctly to begin with. We would definitely use the gift certificate.

We interviewed the owners of two very successful businesses, an auto repair shop, and a frame and body shop. Both owners observed essentially the same thing. Mistakes happen. Most people understand that. The issue is how you deal with the problem when one occurs. Handled poorly, the mistake can result in the loss of a customer. Handled well, the result can be a loyal customer. The key is to accept full responsibility and ensure that you treat the customer more than fairly.

Bernard Robinson, the owner of NTS, a company that provides IT networking support services emphasizes how important it is to make the customer happy when he says, "Fix the customer and the problem, in that order." If a quality issue has affected a customer, you must correct the situation. Provide a replacement. Credit the bill. Give free services. Do whatever is necessary. A quality problem is not a good thing, but handled correctly, it can actually become a positive experience for the customer.

o **Ensure that the problem doesn't persist** – The group processed hundreds of electronic data files each week. They had just discovered that they had processed a duplicate file...again. It would require hours of work to reverse the effects of the mistake and correct all of the accounts. They would do the work to correct the error, just as they had previously, on numerous occasions.

This time there was a difference. For the first time, someone asked another question: "What do we need to do to ensure that this never happens again?" What they needed was a way to identify duplicate files before they processed them.

They decided to change the programming. The new program would compare the first 50 records of each file to the same records of all files the organization received in the past six months. If the program found a match, the file would not be processed pending manual review. When the organization changed the procedure, the processing of duplicate files came to a screeching halt.

Having executed the three prior steps, too many companies call the issue closed. After all, the customer has been satisfied. The urgent issue is resolved, but this approach misses the opportunity to prevent future quality problems. It is imperative to ask, "What caused this problem, and what do we need to do to ensure that it never happens again?" Once you have answered these questions, you can implement the fix.

Midsize businesses should use a common-sense approach to quality improvement.

While following this course of action sounds simple, it requires a disciplined approach and getting the nuances right is critical. But, properly executed, it will put your enterprise on the path to continuous improvement. In the long run, the rewards will be well worth the effort.

o **Cycle time reduction** – If you have a flat on your way home, how long will it take you to change the tire—20 or 30 minutes? How long does it take a mechanic at a Goodyear Tire Store to change a flat—less than five minutes? That's an 80-percent reduction in cycle time. Now ask yourself how long it takes a pit crew to change a tire at Richmond International Raceway. Single-digit seconds per tire? That's more than a 99-percent, cycle-time reduction when compared to the flat tire changer on the side of the road. The opportunities for significant improvements in cycle time are by no means limited to the speedway. Virtually all businesses are good candidates to benefit from this exercise.

Admittedly, the pit crew has specially designed wheels and equipment. They change tires for a living. They practice and they are the best in the world at what they do. Of course, businesses can make the same kinds of investments. For example, we worked with a manufacturer of specialty steel where the average time from accepting an order for a custom alloy to shipment was six months. When we analyzed the time that was absolutely required to schedule and produce the product, it was less than one week. Obviously, there was massive opportunity!

So what must change to reduce cycle times so dramatically? There are many sources of opportunity, but in our experience, the single largest contributor to speeding up processes comes from eliminating or greatly reducing waiting time. Whether it is product working its way through a factory or paperwork moving through a back office, things being processed tend to spend a lot of time waiting. Clearly, wait time adds no value and therefore can be squeezed out.

> **Virtually all businesses are good candidates to benefit from cycle-time reduction.**

Companies often find that processes which have historically been done one after the other (in series) can be done at the same time (in parallel), and therefore, time is saved. For example, pit crews have found that instead of changing tires in series, they can change multiple tires at once.

In some cases, you can design special tools to make the process quicker. Alternatively, dedicated tools can make the job faster. For example, a company that operates injection-molding machines found that they could change the molds faster if the needed wrenches were stored on the same pallet with the molds. This saved the mechanic from having to rummage through his toolbox to find the right wrench—which a coworker had all too often borrowed. It did require purchasing a few more wrenches, but that was a small investment.

Sometimes companies find that they can rework or eliminate portions of their process to reduce cycle time. One company had a quality control step in the middle of a process. However, inspectors almost never found instances of poor quality at that point in the process. Eliminating this QC step saved time and cost almost nothing.

There are many benefits of reducing cycle time. The most obvious benefit is quicker turnaround and shorter lead times. Perhaps more importantly, you can improve quality. Cycle-time reduction almost always results in simplified processes with fewer steps. In most cases, a process that has 10 steps will yield fewer mistakes than a process that has 100 steps. There are just fewer places that things can go wrong. Simpler processes produce fewer errors.

In the same way, you can reduce costs. Simpler processes with fewer steps cost less. You can also reduce waste. Better quality means less scrap and rework. Further, shorter lead times also result in the need to hold less inventory (both work-in-process and finished goods). This means that obsolescence is reduced. Practitioners in the field of lead-time reduction refer to a rule-of-thumb called the ¼-2-20 rule. It states that if you reduce lead times by 25 percent, productivity will double, and you will reduce cost by 20 percent. All of these benefits result in better service, loyal customers, and an improved competitive position.

Ultimately, process improvement will be necessary to enable growth. A process that was completely acceptable when a company operated in a microstructure may be wholly inadequate by the time that same business reaches midsize. In short, businesses will find that to grow they will have to let go of old processes and adopt new ones that are more appropriate to the challenges they face.

When asked if he had documented processes, the owner of a struggling pest control franchise said, "I don't know. Let's look. I've got this manual that headquarters sent me when I bought the business." He obviously didn't know what was inside. Whatever the binder contained, it clearly wasn't doing his business any good. In contrast, when we put the same question to Rusty Smith, the president of Hello Inc., a thriving communications business, he removed three thick binders from the bookshelf behind his desk. You could see the pride on Rusty's face as he placed the binders in front of us on his conference table and said, "That's our company right there."

Documenting process isn't sexy or exciting. No customer will pay more because you have well-documented processes. But, failure to establish appropriate process documentation as a business grows is a recipe for disaster that will result in inconsistent quality, the inability to deliver product and services in a timely manner, and cost overruns. This will result in unhappy customers and frustrated employees. In the long run, good process documentation will have an extremely positive impact on a company's bottom line.

To be sure, this is nontrivial work. It will require a focused and concerted effort on an ongoing basis. While the process of developing this documentation may be challenging, adherence to the following guidelines will ensure that the work goes smoothly.

Lessons for Successful Growth

Recognize the importance of accurate process documentation and ensure that your organization has what it needs to be successful:

- Identify the systems and processes to be documented

- Choose the right person to oversee the documentation

- Ensure that the documentation matches the actual work

- Require that process documentation be a living record

- Ensure continuous improvement

  - Implement a straightforward quality improvement process

  - Reduce cycle times where possible

11: Developing Robust Metrics

Previously, we described a broker/dealer that had been very successful and grown to about 450 financial representatives. Essentially all of the principal's focus had been on sales and marketing. He had never paid appropriate attention to operations. The back office suffered from benign neglect. The company had not documented its processes. They had not automated their back office. It was largely paper based and manual. There was little to no ability to track work on the floor.

No metrics or statistics existed to measure performance. As we were beginning to engage with the company, we asked the person responsible for running the back office to provide us with all of the metrics they used to run the operation. When he responded that there weren't any, we thought that he was being intentionally difficult. Actually, he was just telling the truth.

The company knew it made too many errors, but it had no way to quantify the issue. Standards for service delivery were nonexistent. Again, the company knew that it often took too long to process work, but had no mechanism for quantifying performance. It ran the operation by gut feel and anecdotal evidence. Exasperated financial representatives usually provided the anecdotal evidence by venting their spleen over an error or a delay. Knee-jerk reactions were common.

Good financial representatives had left the company citing poor back office support as one of the reasons for their departure. Unfortunately, without any metrics to measure performance, senior management was "flying blind." They knew things were not good, but they didn't know how bad things really were. They attempted to improve the situation, but without systematic metrics to track results, it was never clear how much progress they made, if any. What they desperately needed was a clear set of metrics with performance standards.

When businesses are very small, owners are typically involved in every aspect of the enterprise. They are aware of all of the details. With a lot of hard work, they increase sales, hire employees, and delegate responsibilities. As the enterprise transitions from a small business to midsize, the principal is no longer familiar with all of the intimate details of the operation. No one could be. There is simply too much going on for one person to get his or her arms completely around. Those charged with responsibility for running the business will need a comprehensive set of metrics to keep them apprised of the enterprise's progress and any issues that may develop.

To be sure, good financial statements are an important part of these metrics. One of the issues we most frequently see in midsize businesses is that the principal needs to recast the financial statements. Without proper financials, the principal won't have the information necessary to make good management decisions. It is critical that the financial information be presented appropriately. However, the business needs more than good financial statements. It will need additional metrics. The principal needs good operating information to make him or her aware of how the business is doing long before the results show up in financial statements. Often, by the time problems are visible on the income statement or the balance sheet, the damage has been done. Developing a robust set of metrics is critical to the operation of any midsize business.

Strange's Florist is an outstanding example of a business that very effectively utilizes metrics. When you walk into President Bill Gouldin's office, you notice there is no clutter. His desk is neat and orderly. Upon closer examination you might also notice a walled-off room in the corner of his office with a locked door. You might think this room to be a large executive bathroom. You'd be wrong.

The room contains the data Bill uses to run his company. If he unlocks that door and lets you peer inside, you'll see stacks of reports; data piled from floor to ceiling. There is a continuous stream of information about the performance of every aspect of the company and Bill scours that data for clues about how to run his business more effectively or efficiently. It's worked. In 1947, Bill's dad and his partner purchased Strange's Florist. They operated the fledgling enterprise in their spare time. But under Bill's leadership, Strange's has grown exponentially. It now ranks as one of the top 25 businesses in FTDs network of over 20,000 florists.

Failure to implement such a set of metrics will inevitably result in one or more of the following:

- **A principal who is completely overwhelmed** – His or her capacity is completely exhausted with running the day-to-day operation of the business because he or she isn't comfortable delegating authority to subordinates. The principal, quite rightly, won't be comfortable delegating authority without good metrics because doing so means losing touch with what is going on in the business. One business owner who had been working day and night, seven days per week for years shared with us that she felt guilty for having taken an evening off to go to a concert.

  This can have a significant adverse impact on the principal's personal life. It's great to love your work and it's great to put a lot of effort into your work. But, when work sucks up every waking second of every day, life gets out of balance. This reduces the quality of life. Left unattended, it will almost certainly have unhappy long-term consequences.

  By the way, even with superhuman effort and the sacrifice of a personal life, if the business continues to grow, there will come a time when the principal simply can't keep up. The business will suffer. Managers in this position need to develop a robust set of metrics so they can delegate responsibilities and lighten their own load (assuming that the right people are already in place and that they have documented processes as discussed previously). Alternatively, the principal could decide to shrink the business to a more manageable size.

- **Stagnant sales** – The senior manager has reached capacity and is unable to do more by himself or herself. Principals who have the discipline to limit the time that they put into their business will eventually find that their businesses stop growing if they don't delegate to others. They become the limiting factor.

We worked with an entrepreneur who would not let go of any significant decision-making responsibility. Therefore, he didn't need many metrics to run his business. He was also religious about not allowing his business to interfere with his personal life. He didn't work weekends. Working past 5:30 was a late night. He spent early evenings with friends and family. The result: stagnant sales—his business's revenue had fluctuated within a fairly narrow range for years.

That's okay, but this should be an explicit decision, not an implicit one. It is completely legitimate for small business owners to decide that they are happy with the size of their business. The principals may be maintaining a good work/life balance and earning enough money to meet their needs. The principals don't want to delegate, so they simply choose not to grow any further.

Business owners in this place would do well to remember one of the primary lessons from Economics 101—when demand exceeds supply, prices go up. If a principal is turning away work, he or she can increase profits without doing more work if he or she raises prices. This will naturally reduce the amount of work that comes to the business, meaning that the business can stay the same size without turning away work. The business is doing the same amount of work, but being paid more for it. Therefore, profits are higher.

- **A business that spirals out of control.** The principal has delegated authority, but he or she lacks insight into what is happening with the business. Some principals who want to grow their business start to experience an unacceptable lifestyle. They become overwhelmed at work and begin to delegate responsibility and authority without having a robust set of metrics with which to manage the business. This is what happened with the broker/dealer described at the beginning of this chapter.

As he or she delegates responsibilities to various employees, the principal begins to lose sight of what is happening in the bowels of the business, because she or he is not personally involved and doesn't have metrics. The managers to whom the principal delegated, although well meaning, will see only part of the picture. They will lack perspective to make decisions that cut across multiple areas of responsibility. With no one to coordinate the managers' efforts, they will inevitably begin to make decisions that are in conflict with each other. The only possible outcome is chaos. Worse, the principal may well not be aware of the underlying issues until they show up in the financial statements. Unfortunately, that's far too late. The damage has already been done.

> **When principals delegate tactical decision-making and management responsibility, they need robust metrics to know what is happening in the bowels of the organization even though they are no longer personally involved in every transaction.**

There comes a point where the business will need a robust set of metrics to enable further growth. The question is how does one design such a set of metrics? In spite of what some pundits may proclaim, our experience shows that there is no "one size fits all" answer to this question. There is no simple formula that will pop out the needed metrics. Each business is different and will require metrics tailored to its specific situation. There are, however, a set of guidelines that can be extremely helpful.

Metrics should:

- Be layered

- Be measurable and stable

- Be Mutually Exclusive and Collectively Exhaustive (MECE)

- Be viewed in context

- Contain checks and balances

- Have point accountability

Metrics should be Layered

An organization of significant size will likely have thousands or even hundreds of thousands of metrics. Senior management should not attempt to review all of the details on a regular basis. If they try, they will become mired in the minutia and not see the forest for the trees. However, it will want to review summarized results and have the ability to drill down to lower levels if an issue is found at the top level.

For example, we worked with a company that had approximately 100 distributors carrying their products. The company also had six different product lines, each with an average of about 1,000 part numbers. If each distributor sells all of every product line, it's easy to see that there are 600,000 different sales numbers to review each month (100 distributors multiplied by six product lines multiplied by 1,000 part numbers per product line). Obviously, reviewing 600,000 different sales numbers each month would quickly become overwhelming.

Senior management should review a summarized, but comprehensive set of metrics with the ability to drill down into more detail if they identify an issue.

Instead, the principal chose to review the overall sales of the company, total sales for each product line, and sales for each of its six geographic sales regions (this represented only 13 sales numbers to scrutinize). Regional sales managers reviewed the sales of each distributor in their region. Product managers reviewed the sales of each part number in their product line. The principal only drilled down to that level of detail when he identified a problem at the top level.

The result is a metrics pyramid as shown below. At the top are a relatively few metrics that the principal reviews, generally a maximum of about 10 pages. Therefore, in less than an hour, the principal can know if there are any issues. If necessary, he or she can drill down into lower layers. At each subsequent level of the organization, there are more detailed metrics, but no one person reviews all of them. The owner can divide the metrics between managers at each level so that no one person has a tremendous burden. Of course, the sum of the metrics reviewed at the lower levels always equal the metrics at higher levels.

Metrics Pyramid

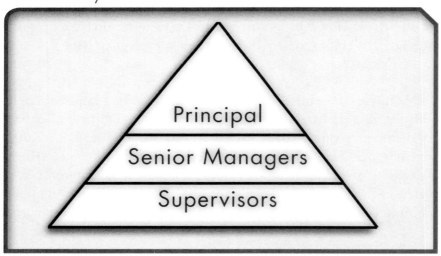

Metrics should be Measurable and Stable

The principal can view measurability on two dimensions: (1) quantitative versus qualitative—things that can be numerically measured versus things that can't, and (2) objective versus subjective—things based on irrefutable fact versus things that are based on opinion. When plotted against each other, the result is the Measurability Matrix shown on page 211.

Measurability Matrix

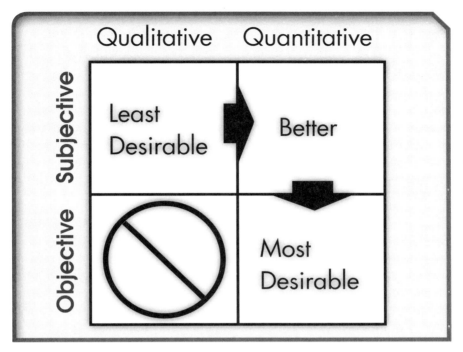

We found no examples of measures that were both Qualitative and Objective (lower left hand quadrant). Sometimes metrics may need to be Qualitative and Subjective. However, this is the least desirable quadrant because there will be disagreement regarding the assessment and whether or not the goal has been achieved. For example, a company may wish to measure how well the senior management team collaborates. Perhaps the best way to accomplish this is for the management team to have an open discussion of how well they are collaborating on a periodic basis. The consensus will be qualitative and subjective. Nevertheless, the fact that the team is focused on how well they work together can lead to improvement.

Even if a measure is inherently subjective, you can often quantify it (moving it from the upper left quadrant to the upper right quadrant). For example, assessing whether a call center employee answers the phone with a pleasant voice is clearly subjective. However, even this subjective measure can be quantified (e.g., the phone was answered pleasantly 98.7 percent of the time).

The most desirable metrics are Quantitative and Objective (the lower right hand quadrant). For example, the dollar sales volume in the northeast region in September would be quantitative and objective. In this quadrant, there can be no argument about the determination of the metric (its objective) and whether or not the goal is achieved will be clear (both the goal and the actual performance are quantified).

Further, the item measured by the principal should be stable. That is, the metric should not vary depending on when he or she takes the measurement. A prosciutto producer measured its inventory in pounds because that's how the product was sold. Unfortunately, there was an issue with stability. During the year it takes to cure prosciutto, the ham's weight falls from around 25 pounds to approximately 12 pounds. The problem is obvious. While the weight of the inventory may be measurable, it is clearly not stable. A much more useful way to measure the inventory, was the number of hams in the curing process. The switch from pounds to number of hams made it much easier to know exactly what was in inventory. Once the prosciutto ham was fully cured, it could be weighed and the inventory of finished product kept in pounds.

A company that recycled scrap metal dealt with instability in a different way. A truck loaded with used soda cans arrives at the scales. It's weighed. The workers offload the cans. Then they weigh the empty truck. The difference between the weight of the full truck and the empty truck is the weight of the cans that the recycler is purchasing. However, that's not the value the company enters into inventory. It knows that some liquid remains in the cans. This accounts for approximately 10 percent of the total weight. Therefore, they allow for this and enter only 90 percent of the weight into inventory. After the employees process the cans, they make an adjustment to account for any error in the approximation.

Metrics should be MECE

Mutually exclusive means that measures at a given level of the hierarchy should not overlap. Each metric should measure one unique thing. For example, "Sales" and "Overhead Expenses" are mutually exclusive. They measure two very different things. "Inventory Turns" and "Days of Inventory On Hand" are not mutually exclusive. They represent two different ways of measuring the same thing. Don't use both. Choose one or the other.

Collectively exhaustive means that, taken together, the metrics at any given level cover all of the important elements of organizational success for which the person at that particular level of the organization is responsible, but no more. Therefore, by definition, a MECE set of metrics is the minimum number of metrics that will give a manager, at a specific level in the hierarchy, a complete view of everything for which she or he is responsible.

Metrics Must be Viewed in Context

In one company, sales in the Northeast Region were $786,549 in May. Is that good news or bad news? Without context, you can't possibly know. However, if we provided you some context and told you that the budget for sales in the Northeast Region for May was $718,000, you would quickly reach the conclusion that the Northeast had a good month in May. Sales exceeded budget by 9.5 percent. This is the value of context.

Context is normally provided by one or more of the following:

• **Budget** is the result the company planned to achieve. How well did we do relative to our plans and goals? For budgets to provide useful context, management must set the numbers at a realistically high level. A budget that is too easy to achieve provides no context because the employees can better it with little to no effort. Exceeding such a budget means nothing. A budget that is set too high is equally worthless because even with super-human effort it isn't attainable. If actual results fall below such a budget, this does not necessarily signify an issue.

  Therefore, to provide useful context, budgets need to be set realistically high. Admittedly, there is an element of judgment associated with determining when a particular budget is realistically high. For this reason, only people who are intimately familiar with the business should establish the budget.

- **History** provides great context because it allows us to see trends. Are we getting better or worse and at what rate? There is often value associated with displaying history as a chart rather than as a table of numbers. Line charts work well in this instance. This makes it much easier for most people to identify trends quickly.

  When using history to provide context, it is important to ensure that you compare apples to apples. For example, a grocery chain might see sales for the month of May up by 10 percent year over year. At first glance, this seems like a good result, but is it a fair comparison? In May a year ago, the chain had 10 stores open. Those same stores are all still open. However, the company opened new stores in July, September, November and February. So, a year-over-year sales growth of 10 percent doesn't seem as impressive when you realize that there are now 40 percent more stores.

  Sometimes you may need to adjust metrics to provide more meaningful context. For example, companies will often compare "same store" sales for a specific period in one year to the same period in the prior year. Such a comparison excludes sales from locations that were not open during both periods. This adjustment makes it clear how sales volume has changed from year to year without having the metric confused by the opening or closing of specific locations.

- **Competition** provides an objective measure of performance. It normalizes for changes in the environment and market conditions that may be beyond the control of the company. Are we gaining ground or losing ground relative to the competition? How has our market share changed over time? Sales may be down by five percent this year. Using only history to provide context, this seems bad. But, if the overall market is down significantly due to a recession, the news may not be so bad after all. If the company's share of market grew from 24 percent to 28 percent during the same time, this five percent decline in sales could actually be viewed as good performance.

In some cases, there are associations that can help provide context by sharing information between companies that compete in the same industry. For example, Toni Gorveatt, COO of Cobb Technologies, a business technology company, explained that her company is a part of the Copier Dealers Association. Because the association is geographically exclusive, none of the members compete directly. Therefore, they share performance information with each other. This data provides great context and allows Toni to understand how Cobb is performing.

Unfortunately, competitive information is not always easily available. When it is, it usually provides the best context. Even without the specific numbers one might have in an ideal world, managers are often able to discern changes in the relative position of competitors.

For example, consider a town that has four residential HVAC servicing companies. One company may well not be able to know the revenue of the other three and therefore precise calculations of market share are impossible. However, they can probably find out fairly easily how many HVAC techs their competitors employ or how many service trucks each has. Sometimes learning this information is as simple as turning up at a competitors shop in the morning and counting the number of cars that pull in and the number of trucks that roll out. If this bit of detective work fails, you can often find out how many techs a competitor employs simply by asking one of its employees. While these numbers won't correlate perfectly with revenue, they are nonetheless a good indicator.

For metrics to be useful, you must view them in appropriate context. It is important to make sure that the reports managers use to run a business provide this.

Metrics Must Contain Checks and Balances

For example, a company might have a goal to increase inventory turns. Viewed by itself, an increase in inventory turns would seem to be a good thing. However, the company can easily obtain this by not ordering any additional product. As a result, on-time deliveries would plummet and stock outs would become rampant. In all probability, this would lead to lost customers and a decline in sales. For an increase in inventory turns to be truly a good thing, the company must balance it by improving on-time deliveries, or at least keeping them steady. In some ways, these checks and balances act as additional context within which to view the metrics.

Similarly, a 25-percent increase in sales in one year would seem to be a good thing. But, if you purchased that sales increase by tripling the size of the sales force, the price may be too high to be profitable. Failure to implement the proper checks and balances can result in counterproductive behavior that goes undetected.

Each Metric Should Have Point Accountability

That is, for each item that is measured, a single person must be accountable—one neck for each metric. For example, consider a P&L that contains the line item "Payroll Expense." Which senior manager is accountable for that line item: the COO, CFO, CIO, VP Sales & Marketing, or VP of Human Resources?

Generally, every senior manager has people in her or his organization. Therefore, every senior manager is, in part, accountable for payroll expense. So, if payroll expense exceeds budget, whom does the CEO hold accountable other than himself or herself? Assuming that the CEO's direct reports each make their own hiring decisions, the answer is that they are all accountable. Unfortunately, when five people are responsible for something, no one is accountable. There is no point accountability, only shared accountability. While assigning more than one person to be responsible for a single metric may be tempting at times, experience has shown that it doesn't work.

It would be much more useful for the CEO to insist that expenses be broken down for each member of the senior management team (e.g., Operations Expense, Finance Expense, IT Expense, Sales & Marketing Expense, HR Expense, etc.). There is then one person accountable for each line item. If there is a problem with one of the metrics, responsibility is clear. Similarly, if performance exceeds expectations, it's clear who gets the credit.

These high-level expense categories can then be broken down further. For example, one of the subdivisions under Sales & Marketing Expense might be Payroll Expense, but it would be clear that the VP of Sales & Marketing is responsible for the Payroll Expense in the Sales & Marketing department.

In our experience, it's amazing how point accountability drives ownership, which in turn results in positive action. In one company with which we worked, after recasting the financial statements and establishing a series of other metrics, the CEO began to conduct monthly meetings where he held his direct reports accountable for the items they owned. At these meetings, the CEO would ask questions such as, "Ron, why is Sales & Marketing Expense seven percent over budget for the month?" In the initial months, Ron's answer was likely to be, "I don't know. I'll find out."

As time passed, the CEO's direct reports became more proactive. They began to provide answers such as, "We were over budget in February because the meeting expense we budgeted in March actually hit in February. We didn't over spend. It's just a timing issue. Next month we will be under budget and our year-to-date numbers will be back in line." Further, because the managers knew they were accountable for not overspending budget, they began to be proactive about managing expenses. Finally, the real magic came at the end of the year when the cost overruns, which had been commonplace in prior years, didn't exist.

For a business to continue growing, the principal must delegate responsibility and authority. To do this effectively, a robust set of metrics must be in place. Developing such a set of metrics requires carefully selecting a MECE set of measures and eliminating others. This can be tricky business, but following the guidelines we outlined will allow the development of an appropriate set of metrics for running any business.

Lessons for Successful Growth

Develop a robust set of metrics for your business by following the steps below. The metrics should:

- **Be layered** – summarized at the top level with more detail at lower levels

- **Be measurable and stable** – objective, quantifiable, and consistent over time

- **Be MECE** – Mutually Exclusive and Collectively Exhaustive

- **Be viewed in context** – provided by budget, history, and/or competitive performance

- **Contain checks and balances** – so that unbalanced improvements don't cause more harm than good

- **Have point accountability** – only one person who is responsible for results

Summary

In the course of our research for this book, we spoke with more than 100 principals of micro, small and midsize businesses. We spent untold hours listening to their stories of success and failure, triumph, and frustration. We coupled what we heard with our own years of experience managing businesses. We confirmed what we knew. Growing a business is hard work and a lot of successful companies plateau well short of their potential. We also learned that the most frequent constraint to growing a business is not access to capital, market opportunity or good ideas. No, we found that what most often limits the growth of small businesses is the inability or unwillingness of principals to let go.

At first it may seem surprising, but not all business owners want to grow their businesses. Depending on what the owner wants to accomplish, not growing the company can be a good decision. However, if the owner does decide to grow the business, the enterprise will inevitably face a predictable set of challenges. While you can't avoid them all together, it is possible to take actions that will allow you to continue to grow your business by appropriately addressing them. As the chart below shows, when the business migrates from micro to small and subsequently from small to midsize, the principal must accept new responsibilities. Perhaps more importantly, she or he will also have to give up certain responsibilities at each step in the process. The principal will have to *Let Go to Grow*.

As a micro business, the principal does the primary work of the enterprise. Many entrepreneurs go into business because they are very good at doing the primary work of the business and they genuinely enjoy it. At this stage, the success of the company is largely a function of how well the principal can do this work. Beyond this, she or he will have to establish strategy for the business and make day-to-day tactical decisions.

For the business to make the transition from micro to small successfully, the principal will have to let go of the primary work of the business. Others will need to assume this responsibility. Some principals don't want to stop doing the primary work of the business; they are good at it, they love it, and they want to keep doing it. That's fine, but to grow her or his business beyond the size that a micro business structure will support, the principal must let go. When that happens, his or her skills as a manager become more important than his or her ability to do the primary work of the business. Making good tactical decisions and establishing strategy remain the principal's responsibility. In addition, he or she will have to get the right workers into the right roles and become good at managing those people.

When the business moves from small to midsize, the principal has to delegate authority for hiring and managing at least some of the workers and making at least some of the tactical decisions. At the same time, he or she must hold the people who accept these responsibilities accountable for the performance of those they manage.

Worse than not delegating, is doing so before you have laid the proper groundwork. The principal must ensure that the right managers are in place. In addition, they will need to document their processes, establish systems, and develop appropriate metrics. For many principals, the transition from small to midsize is more difficult than the transition from micro to small. Relinquishing decision-making authority equals giving up control. This is often difficult for people who have been successful precisely because they were good at controlling things. It's always difficult to give up doing the things that have made you successful in the past. But, to effectively grow the business, the principal must let go.

Principal's Responsibilities

	Micro	Small	Midsize
Doing the work of the business	✓	⊘	
Make tactical decisions	✓	✓	⊘
Develop strategy	✓	✓	✓
Get the right workers in the right jobs		✓	⊘
Manage workers		✓	⊘
Delegate Authority and Hold Accountable			✓
Get the Right Managers in Place			✓
Establish Systems and Document Processes			✓
Develop Robust Metrics			✓

As a business transitions from one stage to the next, the principal must morph his or her skill set. This is a significant challenge. The good news is that these are learned skills. A principal who is committed to making the transition can do so if they know where they want to go. Principals can learn how to let go safely so that their businesses can grow!

Postscript: Take Wise Counsel

We've often heard principals of small or midsize companies express their reticence to hire a consultant because they think managing the company is their job and they shouldn't need help. Yet, Michael Phelps has a swim coach, the Williams sisters make use of tennis coaches, and Nolan Ryan had a pitching coach. While these athletes are or were among the best in their respective sports, their coaches have helped make them better than they would have been on their own.

When you think about it, it's not hard to understand why principals could benefit from wise counsel. The set of skills that it takes to run a micro business, where the principal is the only employee, is very different from the skill set needed to manage a robust midsize business with $125 million in revenue and 250 employees. You aren't born with the skills needed to run such a company. You have to learn them. Many entrepreneurs are smart, hardworking people. They will eventually figure out how to manage a midsize business successfully through trial and error. Unfortunately, the trials will be difficult and the errors expensive. There is no reason to reinvent the wheel.

> **The set of skills it takes to run a micro business are fundamentally different from the skills required to manage a midsize enterprise.**

If you want to design and build a house, you could start from scratch. You could learn how thick footings should be by trial and error. You could discover on your own how residential electrical wiring and plumbing work. You could buy a book and try to figure out the functioning of an HVAC system, but you wouldn't.

You'd begin by talking to an architect or a contractor. You'd learn what is possible and what isn't, what costs too much, what is unsafe, and what options are available. You'd take advantage of centuries of accumulated knowledge regarding how to build a house. The house would still be your house. You wouldn't abdicate decisions about the square footage of the house, how many bedrooms and bathrooms would be in the house, what appliances would go into the kitchen, or what chandelier to hang in the foyer. You would still own the critical decisions, but you would seek help from experts regarding the details of the infrastructure.

Running a midsize business is much more complex than building a house. When making important decisions, benefit from the mistakes and successes of others. Build on the accumulated knowledge that already exists. Seek the help of experts. By definition, entrepreneurs are people who like to go it alone and do things on their own. They are not afraid to take risks. In this case, resist the temptation. It's the smart thing to do. Take wise counsel.

The CEOs of the world's largest and most successful companies routinely engage management consulting firms such as McKinsey, Bain, BCG, or Booz Allen. Again, these CEOs are among the most gifted and accomplished people in their fields. Many have MBAs from top-tier business schools. All have years of experience and, yet, they hire consultants to help their companies to become more successful.

Clearly some of the most accomplished people in sports and in business see value in external counsel. The issues are:

- How does a good consultant create value for a competent manager?
- How should a manager select a consultant with whom to work?
- How can a manager work most effectively with a consultant?

We will address these questions in this postscript.

How Consultants Create Value

A good management consultant can deliver value in many ways. We have outlined a few of these below.

- **Functional Expertise** – For many consultants, at least some portion of their practice is expertise based. The consultant possesses knowledge that the manager simply does not have. Frequently this expertise is in some functional area that is not core to the business. For example, we performed an audit of the human resources practices and procedures for an HVAC installation and service company. While HR is important in every business, it certainly was not core to the work of this firm.

The company was not large enough to be able to afford a highly qualified senior HR professional and therefore, senior management wasn't certain that it complied with all of the necessary, but complex, employment regulations. Because the company employed more than 50 people, it was required to comply with most of the same regulations that would apply to a Fortune 500 company. The audit revealed that the company was largely in compliance. However, it was deficient in a couple of critical areas. There were also several other areas where, although not out of compliance, the company was not following best practices and, therefore, was leaving itself open to potential liability.

At a relatively small cost, the HVAC firm was able to implement new policies and procedures that ensured it complied with all applicable regulations. The company also improved its HR practices on a number of dimensions. Further, they trained their managers and supervisors to implement these new procedures and protect the assets of the company.

Had regulators discovered the compliance issues before the company corrected them, it could have faced fines and penalties that would have made the consulting fees they paid look inconsequential. Further, it would not have been reasonable for this midsize company to increase its payroll by hiring a full-time senior HR professional with the knowledge to identify and correct these issues. There simply wasn't enough work for such a person on an ongoing basis. Hiring a consultant was a much more cost-effective solution.

- **Process-Based Expertise** – The consultant's expertise may also be process-based. For example, the consultant may have expertise in facilitating the strategic planning process. The consultant won't have nearly as much industry or company specific knowledge as the manager, but she or he will have taken companies through the strategic planning process many times. The manager knows her or his industry and company exceedingly well, but has developed relatively few robust strategic plans. Working together, the consultant and the manager can develop a much better strategic plan for the business than either could working alone.

- **Industry-Based Expertise** – Some consultants have a wealth of experience in a single, narrowly focused industry. Such experts can often walk through an operation and make valuable suggestions in very short order. We know of a company that has very successfully built and operated cold storage warehouses around the world. They started a consulting practice to help others improve the operation of their cold storage warehouses. This firm adds value based on its decades of experience in the industry.

- **Objective Third Party** – A good consultant can also play the role of an objective third party. Such a person brings several things to the table:

  o First, because the consultant is not a part of the company, they are more likely to be able to get completely candid responses from junior employees than would senior management. It's often not easy for an employee to tell senior management "their baby's ugly." They keep their thoughts to themselves. There is real value in hearing what the rank and file employees think about the business. However, frequently the only way employees will share their thoughts candidly is when they are talking to someone who can't fire them, discipline them, or withhold pay increases and promotions.

There's a reality television show where the senior managers of very large companies pose as new, entry-level employees. When the front line workers candidly share their perspective with their "new co-worker," the senior manager often experiences a revelation about how to run his or her business more effectively. The principals in small or midsize companies can't get away with this. Everyone in the company knows who they are. But, an objective third party can elicit the same kind of candid information from front-line employees.

o   Second, when a manager has been working in a business for a long time, he or she can become blind to new and different ways of doing things. The French call this, *la deformation professionnelle*. It translates as "the professional deformation" and refers to the way that companies can lock their managers into certain ways of doing things or certain ways of thinking. It's been said that the last seven words uttered in many failing businesses are, "We have always done it this way." It often takes a person from outside the business to see significant opportunities.

We worked with an electronics distributor that had a significant problem managing its inventory. One of the big issues they faced was that lead times could go from two weeks to as much as six months without notice. If the manufacturer had the product in stock, the lead-time was two weeks or less. If the manufacturer stocked out of a particular part number, the part was back ordered and delivery could not be made until the next production run which might be many months in the future. On one hand, the distributor couldn't afford to lose sales because they were out of stock, but on the other hand, the cost of carrying enough inventory to cover for the lead-time swings was prohibitive.

It turns out that suppliers would allow the company to place orders up to six months in advance. Once the company placed an order, the manufacturer would allocate stock to that order. There was no penalty for cancelling all or part of an order as long as the company did so at least 30 days in advance of delivery. We devised an inventory management system where the company placed monthly orders six months in advance for 20 percent more than the distributor thought it would need. Thirty-one days prior to receipt of an order, the distributor would simply cancel whatever part of the order it didn't need.

Therefore, the mechanism for managing inventory wasn't placing orders, as is normally the case, but rather cancelling the portion it did not need. Since cancellation occurred consistently at 31 days prior to shipment, in effect this locked in a 31-day lead-time. Since there was always a pipeline of orders due to arrive 30 days apart, there was no longer a problem with lead times increasing without notice.

This innovative way to manage inventory worked because of the specific rules that the manufacturers created. However, it is unlikely that anyone at the client would have thought to do things in this out-of-the-box way, not because they weren't smart, but because they were so close to how they had always done things.

o Finally, remember that employees may be reticent to share negative thoughts with senior management even in a constructive manner. On the other hand, a part of the value that a good consultant brings is that he or she can be completely candid regarding the shortcomings of a business or indeed of the senior managers themselves.

It was the famous 18th-century Scottish poet Robert

Burns who observed, "Oh, that God would give us the very smallest of gifts. To be able to see ourselves as others see us. It would save us from many mistakes and foolish thoughts." (Translated from *To a Louse*) Burns had it right. There can be real value to an unbiased assessment from an objective third party. It sometimes takes an outsider to point out that "the emperor has no clothes" even if everyone other than the emperor can see that fact clearly.

- **Accountability Coach** – In many businesses, senior managers find that the urgent overwhelms the important. For example, monthly reviews of progress made against objectives laid out in the annual strategic plan are very important. Unfortunately, in many companies these meetings never happen because there are always more urgent things that need to be accomplished. However, if an outside consultant is scheduling and facilitating monthly reviews of the strategic plan, the meetings are much more likely to occur. The consultant becomes an accountability coach who helps the managers do those important things they know they should do, but might otherwise never manage to find time to get done.

- **Focused Talent** – Managers often find that it's difficult to assign their most talented people to special projects. That's because the best people are intimately involved in the day-to-day operation of the business, as well they should be. So, when the need for a special project arises, say some in-depth competitive analysis for example, it can be tough to have top performers committed to the task on a full-time basis. The result is either the company assigns a mediocre player to these important special projects or they ask top performers to handle them off the side of their desks. In either case, the result is unlikely to be what the company needs. Hiring a smart, experienced, creative consultant to focus on such tasks can often pay real dividends.

- **Managing Transitions** – When a company transitions from a micro business to a small business, the principal is required to do a series of things that have not been important previously.

The same is true when the business grows from a small business to a midsize business. If the principal lacks experience with these new skills, he or she can find himself or herself reinventing the wheel.

Because the principal is bright, motivated, and hardworking, she or he will eventually figure out what works. However, with no clear road map and little knowledge of what has worked and not worked in other companies, this will inevitably be a trial and error process. Mistakes will be made along the way,

Good consultants can add value through:
- **Functional expertise**
- **Processed based expertise**
- **Industry based expertise**
- **Being an objective third party**
- **Acting as an accountability coach**
- **Providing focused talent**
- **Managing transitions**

some potentially quite costly. In the best case, finding the right path will take time and the company will pay an opportunity cost. A knowledgeable and experienced consultant can significantly increase the speed of these transitions. In the process, the principal will save significant money and avoid much aggravation.

Selecting a Consultant

Results-driven counsel can be unbelievably helpful and deliver value that is many times the cost, but poor counsel can be disastrous. For example, we worked with one company where a previous consultant, a professor from a well-known college, had convinced management to put all of their warehouse and factory workers on salary. The result was that these employees received a salary that was 30 percent larger than what they would previously have received for working a full 40-hour week.

However, the consultant justified the pay increase by explaining that the company wouldn't have to pay overtime. He explained that because these workers would be on self-directed work teams, they would be exempt from the requirement that they receive time-and-a-half pay for overtime. This advice was simply wrong. It put the company in violation of wage and hour regulations. It turns out that companies must pay their frontline workers overtime whether or not they are self-directed. It's the law. The employees were unquestionably not exempt. Upon learning this, management had to reverse the decision. The employees, not surprisingly, viewed the change in compensation as a pay reduction. What resulted was not pretty. The company's experience with this consultant was not a positive one.

The moral of the above story is that choosing the right consultant is critical. In selecting a consultant, it makes sense to follow a few simple, but important guidelines. Choose a consultant who has:

- **Unimpeachable Character** – First and foremost, an effective consultant must be a person of the highest character. He or she must be the consummate professional. The consultant must be willing to put the best interest of the client ahead of his or her own interests. For example, the consultant must be willing to tell clients things they need to hear, but may not want to hear—even if telling the client means that the consultant loses business. The consultant must care deeply about her or his clients. We say, "We will walk through fire for our clients." What we mean is that, within ethical limits, we are willing to do whatever it takes to help them succeed.

- **Solid Experience** – A good consultant should have experience with the challenges or opportunities you and your company are facing. She or he may not know your specific company or industry, but you and your people know your company and your industry quite well. What the consultant brings to the table is experience in addressing the types of issues you face. For example, if you are seeking help in setting up an inventory management system, you will want to make sure the consultant you engage has worked with inventory management processes previously. Beyond functional expertise, make sure the consultant you hire has a proven record of success. Ask for references and check them. It's better not to have a consultant who is learning on your nickel.

- **Creative Problem-Solving Skills** – You will want the consultant you engage to be an outstanding problem solver. After all, you are hiring a consultant to help you solve problems (or take advantage of opportunities). Marvin Bower, the patriarch of McKinsey & Company, essentially founded management consulting. In the process, he grew the firm from a fledgling enterprise to a global operation. Outlining his criteria for an outstanding consultant, Bower wrote, "Mental equipment — The successful consultant has outstanding analytical skill and the ability to synthesize his thoughts readily in reaching conclusions. He is a quick and effective learner—imaginative and creative." A McKinsey partner with whom we worked said, "Marvin had it right; you've got to start with raw horsepower." When choosing a consultant, make sure to hire superior problem solvers.

- **Outstanding Communication Skills** – A good consultant should be articulate. He or she should possess unusually strong communication skills, both orally and in writing. Of course, communication is a two-way street. Perhaps, more important than their ability to speak articulately and write eloquently is their ability to listen. No matter how smart a consultant is, she or he won't be able to help you improve your business until she or he fully understands the challenges you face. This will never happen until the consultant listens to you. That's why, when you ask a good consultant what he or she can do for you, the response will always be, "Before I can answer that, I'll need you to tell me a little bit about your business." Only after the consultant has listened can she or he really explain the best way to improve your business.

- **Excellent Interpersonal Skills** – Simply put, for any consultant to be successful in helping your company, a trust-based relationship is going to have to develop. You will need to be comfortable revealing the intimate details of your business to this person. The relationship between consultant and client is not unlike the relationship between a doctor and patient. Without complete candor, the consultant will be hindered in his or her effort to help your business. Choose a consultant with whom you can develop this kind of professional relationship.

Choose a consultant with:
- **Unimpeachable character**
- **Solid experience**
- **Creative problem-solving skills**
- **Strong communication skills**
- **Excellent interpersonal skills**

If you engage a consultant who possesses these five characteristics, you will receive value that greatly exceeds the cost.

Working Effectively with a Consultant

If you've decided to invest your company's money in working with a consultant and you have identified the consultant, it only makes sense to make certain you get maximum benefit from the work. Here are a few tips for ensuring success when you work with a consultant:

- **Make the Project a Priority** – If you are working with a good consultant, you will need to commit significant time, effort, and resources to ensure a successful engagement. You should only do this if the upside potential greatly exceeds the cost. Our rule of thumb is that the potential benefit should be at least 10 times the cost. If you follow this rule, and if you work well with a competent consultant, you are most likely to achieve benefit that will exceed the cost.

- **Provide Access to People and Resources** – To be effective, the consultant will need access to you, your people, and the information that resides in your organization. Be prepared to have your IT person provide the necessary data. Ensure that your CFO or CPA provides appropriate financial information. Make certain that your people are available for interviews, brainstorming sessions, and to serve on taskforces.

- **Commit to do the Required Work** – The old adage, "You only get out of something what you put into it" is almost universally true. Working with a management consultant is not an exception to this rule. To derive full benefit, you will have to invest some time and effort. Remember the consultant brings a lot to the table, but he or she will not generally know your company and industry as well as you do. The most successful engagements are collaborative partnerships. Most consultants will ask you and your team to work with them.

  Before you agree to the engagement, make sure you understand what the consultant will require and that you are prepared to invest that level of effort. We live in the real world and emergencies happen. At the same time, the consulting engagement is very important; if it isn't, don't do it. The urgent is always the enemy of the important. If you allow yourself and/or your team to get away without doing the necessary work, the results will be disappointing.

- **Be Open and Honest** – For a consultant to do your company the maximum amount of good, she or he will need to understand the full picture. You wouldn't go to a doctor and misrepresent your symptoms or knowingly leave important information out. If you did, you couldn't reasonably expect to have your condition correctly diagnosed and treated. In the same way, you are going to have to be completely open and honest with your consultant. He or she is there to help you, not to judge you. In order to be comfortable doing this, you are going to have to develop a trust-based relationship with your consultant. That's why it is important to select a consultant with whom you are comfortable.

- **Don't Abdicate the Management of Your Company** – As much value as a good consultant can deliver, the traditional way in which consultants work with their clients has at least one major drawback. The old joke goes that consultants are people who take your watch to tell you the time. It's funny only because there's some truth to it. Typically, consultants will request a lot of data, interview a lot of people, and gather a lot of company documents. They'll collect all of this information, conduct a great deal of analysis and come back with a series of recommendations. Unfortunately, the client may or may not be completely committed to executing the consultant's recommendations. After all, they are "the consultant's recommendations," not the management team's. If the team isn't 100 percent committed, the results are sure to be less than completely satisfactory.

  > **To work effectively with a consultant:**
  > - **Make the project a priority**
  > - **Provide access to people and resources**
  > - **Commit to do the required work**
  > - **Be open and honest**
  > - **Don't abdicate management of your company**

  It's critical for the client to own the action steps. A better way for consultants to function is to work with management by questioning them, pushing their thinking, and presenting new ideas, concepts, and analysis. But, when it's time to develop the action steps, its management that must own them. The business will be much better off with a plan to which management is 100 percent committed. Good consultants can be of tremendous value, but it's critical that management not abdicate responsibility for deciding the direction of the business.

If you are going to work with a consultant, be prepared to make the necessary commitment to achieve success.

The effective use of a good consultant can create significant value. Choosing the wrong consultant with whom to work or not engaging with your consultant in a constructive way can be value destroying. Following the above guidelines will help to ensure that you select the right consultant and that your company garners full value from the engagement.

Lessons for Successful Growth

Recognize the growth stage of your company. Is your business transitioning? Given the stage of your business, do you have the infrastructure you need? Are the right people in place? Does your business have the documented processes and the metrics it needs?

If your business is lacking on some dimension, recognize your own strengths and weaknesses. Do you have experience shepherding a business through the midsize stage? Would you and your business benefit from outside help? If so, ask for that help. It's important for the success of your business.

Acknowledgements

A large number of people generously contributed to the development of *Let Go to Grow*. We are greatly indebted to them. First, we wish to sincerely thank those who shared the intimate details of their businesses with us – the triumphs and disappointments of their life's work. They shared their inspiring stories and as our thinking began to emerge, allowed us to bounce our ideas off them. Their input forms the basis of this book and the core of our thinking. In addition to providing us with their insight, many of these business leaders also introduced us to other people that we interviewed. We promised not to publish a list of their names or their companies. Of course, we will honor that commitment. But, this in no way diminishes our gratitude to these very generous people.

We would like to give a special thanks to the many people that opened doors for us and enabled us to gain access to the wonderful business owners who provided input to this project. This group includes: Marian Alderson, Nancy Boyer, Julia Boykin, Bob Bremer, Alex Cherlin, JC Corrigan, Beth Johnson, Teri Mackey, John Meacham, With Michael, Gary Rhoades, Logan Ryan, Kim Sheeler, Chris Shouldice, and Stephanie Wall. There help made our work much easier and enabled us to produce a better product.

David Smitherman, our publisher, did a wonderful job of shepherding us through this process. Many meetings lasted well into the evening hours. We appreciate his dedication and commitment to the project. Without him, *Let Go to Grow* would not have been possible. We would also like to thank Sarah Lapallo for designing and formatting the book.

We wish to thank Emily Rush, our assistant, for her contribution. She spent untold hours calling people to request interviews, scheduling appointments and then rescheduling them when the real world overtook our plans. Without her tireless effort, this work would have been much more difficult and would have taken much longer. We thank Emily for her efforts.

We are grateful to Dave Saunders, Joel Abercrombie and Stephanie Derry from Madison + Main for their creative leadership, marketing ideas and for orchestrating the cover design. We are also thankful to the other Madison + Main staff members, especially the creative team, who worked behind the scenes to make this happen.

We are indebted to a large number of business leaders who read our work and provided input, feedback and comments. They spent untold hours poring over unedited manuscripts and helped us refine our thinking. That group includes: Rick Batty, David Bratt, Bob Bremer, Jerry Bricker, Doug Brown, Bruce Bruinsma, John Clendenin, Mark Creery, Chris Daifotis, Monica Dodi, Mark Flynn, Jack Frost, Ben Gajewski, Doug Gernert, Jim Godshall, Tony and Teri Gutierrez, Greville Hampson, Bill Helman, John Helmoe-Zinck, Steve Kaufman, Dorian Klein, Kim Lopdrup, Gerry Lopez, Paul Maeder, Susan McGhee, Sharon Medere, Marc Meyer, Tony Meyer, Mark Nunnelly, Rene Robichaud, Dave Saunders, Mark Sullivan, Kim Scheeler, Bob Sulentic, Tom Temple, Reggie Van Lee, John Weber, Steve Wiggins, and Kathy Wollum. Their help was invaluable. To each of these people we are truly grateful.

Finally, we offer a word of thanks to the many family members, friends and business acquaintances that let us bounce our ideas off them and provided informal feedback and words of encouragement.

Index

Book Order Form

Telephone Orders: Call (866) 570-6724

Fax Orders: (866) 570-6724

Postal Orders: Palari Publishing, PO Box 9288, Richmond, VA 23227

Website: WhitestonePartnersInc.com

Email: orders@palaribooks.com

Please send the following:

_____ Let Go to GROW book @ $24.95 each
number of books

Company:_____

Name: _____

Address: _____

City: _____

State:_____ ZIP: _____

Phone:_____

Email: _____

Payment:

Check | Money Order | Credit Card

Card Number: _____

Name on Card:_____

Ex. Date:_____

Signature: _____

Shipping and Handling:

USA only: $6.00 for first book, $3.00 for each additional book
(Virginia residents add 5% sales tax.)